FAVORITE BRAND NAME™

Classroom Treats

D1405227

Publications International, Ltd.

Favorite Brand Name Recipes at www.fbnr.com

Pictured on the front cover: Glazed Donut Cookies *(page 212).*
Pictured on the back cover *(left to right):* Brontosaurus Bites *(page 30)* and Rainbow Spirals *(page 194).*

ISBN-13: 978-1-4127-2159-2
ISBN-10: 1-4127-2159-8

Library of Congress Control Number: 2004113590

Manufactured in China.

8 7 6 5 4 3 2 1

Microwave Cooking: Microwave ovens vary in wattage. Use the cooking times as guidelines and check for doneness before adding more time.

Preparation/Cooking Times: Preparation times are based on the approximate amount of time required to assemble the recipe before cooking, baking, chilling or serving. These times include preparation steps such as measuring, chopping and mixing. The fact that some preparations and cooking can be done simultaneously is taken into account. Preparation of optional ingredients and serving suggestions is not included.

Contents

Lifesaving Tips for Room Moms

*W*hether you volunteered to be a room mom or just offered to bring the treats, let *Classroom Treats* come to the rescue. With a little planning, classroom parties and celebrations will be fun for kids and easy on busy moms. Experienced classroom moms offer the following advice.

Popular Treats

Make your party a spectacular success by bringing treats kids love most. Survey teachers, students and parents to discover the most popular treats.

- Believe it or not, beverages such as punch with sherbet or ice cream, root beer floats and fun, fizzy drinks are all the rage. Look for delicious ideas on pages 6 to 17.
- Snack mixes also receive rave reviews and the combinations are endless. Find a multitude of ingredients and flavors for crunchy mixes on pages 18 to 39. These finger foods will always be a hit.
- For a last-minute treat, ask each student to bring a box of their favorite snack—cereal, dried fruits, miniature crackers, pretzels or marshmallows. Put each ingredient in a separate bowl. Add serving spoons and give each student a cup to mix their very own crunchy mix.

- Name treats with whimsical titles to match the party theme and add to the excitement.

Serve more than the kids!

Be sure to check with the teacher to determine the number of servings to prepare. Plan for at least 30 and always allow for extra staff and parents. The principal, room assistants and parent helpers often attend class parties.

Party Tips—Make it Easy!

Colored or party-themed plates, napkins, fancy straws and disposable utensils not only create a festive party atmosphere but—even more important for the room mom— make cleanup a breeze. Even the simplest snacks served on decorative plates add fun to the celebration.

- Think small sizes when selecting paper party goods. Child-size utensils and plates make snacks easier to hold and eat. And, small cups and plates help control serving sizes.
- When party time is short, package and serve snack mixes or cookies in themed goodie bags for easy-to-serve treats.
- Bring food storage bags to pack up leftover treats for take-home goodie bags.

- For special parties, customize party treats with a theme. Delightful novelty cookies and cakes (see pages 40 to 141) add excitement to the celebration. Choose from a wealth of ideas on how to transform plain treats into magical themed cakes and cookies.

Better Food Choices for Kids

Party food can be delicious and nutritious at the same time. Look for recipes on pages 142 to 175. Also, try one of the following suggestions to make reduced sugar and fat versions of snacks that tempt appetites with colorful tasty treats.

- Reduce sugar consumption by making delicious snack cakes or cupcakes without the frosting. Tasty muffins are also a good choice.
- Make smaller-sized cookies, cakes and muffins. Often one mini cupcake or cookie is the perfect size snack—tummies are filled and food is not wasted. Of course, seconds are always available.
- Prepare a decorative platter with an assortment of cut-up fruits and vegetables or crackers and cheese cubes to serve with sugary treats.
- Incorporate shredded or mashed fruits and vegetables into cookies, cakes and cupcakes whenever possible. Shredded zucchini or carrots, applesauce or mashed bananas add moisture but less sugar and fat without sacrificing flavor. Vegetables in cake! No one will ever know.

- Don't be afraid to prepare savory treats like mini sandwiches, pizzas and rollers and wraps (see pages 176 to 199). These appetizing finger foods will be gobbled up in minutes.

Special Diets

Ask the teacher about school policies and special dietary needs of the children. If there are food or beverage restrictions due to diabetes or food allergies such as milk, wheat or peanuts, follow these simple tips:

- When making special food snacks, prepare that same item for the entire class. Avoid making special snacks for just one or two children. Look for kid-favorite recipes that will fit a variety of special food needs on pages 142 to 171.
- Serve ice water as one of the beverage choices at every party.

Last-Minute Recipes

For busy moms, sometimes simple is best. Check out pages 200 to 217 for treats to prepare at a moment's notice.

Make children's parties spectacular. This book is designed to help you throw creative, memorable parties— the best they've ever seen!

Liquid Potions

Start out the party with colorful thirst-quenching beverages. Mix up tasty fruit juices and top with ice cream or sherbet for foamy, bubbling concoctions.

Bobbing Head Punch

Assorted candies
Assorted fruit slices and pieces
Water
6 cups white grape juice
2 cups apple juice or 2 additional cups ginger ale
4 cups ginger ale
Green food coloring

1. Arrange candy and fruit pieces in bottom of 9-inch glass pie plate to create a face. (Remember, the bottom of the face is what will show in the punch bowl.)

2. Add water to cover face and carefully place in freezer. Freeze overnight.

3. At time of serving, combine grape juice, apple juice and ginger ale to 4- to 5-quart punch bowl. Tint mixture green. Invert pie plate, placing one hand underneath. Run the plate under cold running water to release frozen face. Place ice mold upside down on top of juice mixture and serve.

Makes 20 cups

Party Preparation Tip: The ice ring will melt slightly while transporting to the classroom. Instead of running the pie plate under cold water, place one hand over the frozen face and invert the pie plate. The ice mold will immediately release. Carefully place over the juice mixture.

Dripping Blood Punch

8 thick slices cucumber
4 cups pineapple juice
1 cup orange juice
2 cups ginger ale or sparkling water
   Ice
8 tablespoons grenadine syrup

1. Cut cucumber slices into vampire fangs as shown in photo.

2. Combine pineapple and orange juices in large pitcher. Refrigerate until serving time.

3. Immediately before serving, stir ginger ale into juices. Fill clear plastic cups generously with ice; add vampire fangs to rims. Pour punch into ice-filled cups. Slowly drizzle 1 tablespoon grenadine over top of each serving. *Makes 8 servings*

Hot Cocoa with Floating Eyeballs

16 large marshmallows
16 black licorice candies
2 quarts milk
1 cup chocolate-flavored drink mix
1 cup mint-flavored semisweet chocolate chips

● Make slit in center of each marshmallow; insert licorice candy into slit. Set aside.

● Combine milk and drink mix in medium saucepan. Stir in chocolate chips. Cook over medium heat, stirring occasionally, until chips are melted and milk is heated through. Pour mixture into large thermos to carry to school.

● To serve, place 2 eyeballs in each cup; fill cup with hot cocoa. Serve immediately. *Makes 8 cups*

Dripping Blood Punch ✗ 9

Magic Potion

    Creepy Crawler Ice Ring (recipe follows)
  1 **cup boiling water**
  2 **packages (4-serving size each) lime-flavored gelatin**
  3 **cups cold water**
1½ **quarts carbonated lemon-lime beverage, chilled**
 ½ **cup superfine sugar**
    Gummy worms (optional)

1. One day ahead, prepare Creepy Crawler Ice Ring.

2. Pour boiling water over gelatin in heatproof punch bowl; stir until gelatin dissolves. Stir in cold water. Do not refrigerate or jello will harden. Just before serving, add lemon-lime beverage and sugar; stir well (mixture will foam for several minutes). Unmold ice ring by dipping bottom of mold briefly into hot water. Float ice ring in punch. Serve cups of punch garnished with gummy worms, if desired.

Makes about 10 cups

Creepy Crawler Ice Ring

  1 **cup gummy worms or other creepy crawler candy**
  1 **quart lemon-lime thirst quencher beverage**

Arrange gummy worms in bottom of 5-cup ring mold; fill mold with thirst quencher beverage. Freeze until solid, 8 hours or overnight.

Makes 1 ice ring

Make It Special

Kids love foaming beverages. Sherbet or ice cream will foam when a carbonated drink is poured over them. You can also create foam by adding a carbonated beverage and sugar to the punch bowl. To get the best effect, be sure to add these ingredients just before serving.

Hot Chocolate

- **2 cups nonfat milk**
- **8 packets SPLENDA® No Calorie Sweetener**
- **3 tablespoons powdered cocoa (preferably Dutch processed)**

Garnish
- **¼ teaspoon cinnamon**
- **2 tablespoons reduced-calorie whipped topping**

PLACE milk in small saucepan. Mix contents of SPLENDA® Packets and cocoa powder in small bowl. Add to milk and whisk well. Simmer 4 to 5 minutes over medium-low heat until steaming.

POUR mixture into 2 serving cups. Optional garnish: Top each with 1 tablespoon reduced-calorie whipped topping and pinch of ground cinnamon.

Makes 2 cups

Prep Time: 10 minutes

Ghastly Glow Punch

- **Fruit leathers**
- **2 quarts ginger ale**
- **2 cups cranberry juice cocktail concentrate**
- **2 cups mango, orange or peach sherbet or sorbet**

1. Using Halloween or other holiday cookie cutters, cut shapes out of fruit leathers; place in covered plastic container.

2. To serve, combine ginger ale and cranberry juice concentrate in serving bowl. Drop sherbet by tablespoonfuls into punch. Sprinkle shapes over sherbet or use to garnish punch cups. Serve immediately.

Makes 12 cups

Golden Harvest Punch

- 4 cups MOTT'S® Apple Juice
- 4 cups orange juice
- 3 liters club soda
- 1 quart orange sherbet
- 5 pound bag ice cubes (optional)

Combine apple juice, orange juice and club soda in punch bowl. Add scoops of sherbet or ice. *Makes about 25 cups*

"Lemon Float" Punch

- Juice of 10 to 12 SUNKIST® lemons (2 cups)
- ¾ cup sugar
- 4 cups water
- 1 bottle (2 liters) ginger ale, chilled
- 1 pint lemon sherbet or frozen vanilla yogurt
- Lemon half-cartwheel slices and fresh mint leaves (optional) for garnish

Combine lemon juice and sugar; stir to dissolve sugar. Add water; chill. To serve, in large punch bowl, combine lemon mixture and ginger ale. Add small scoops of sherbet, lemon slices and mint, if desired. *Makes about 15 cups*

Raspberry Sherbet Punch

- 1 to 2 liters HAWAIIAN PUNCH® Fruit Juicy Red
- 4 cups club soda
- 4 cups ginger ale
- 2 cups water
- 4 cups raspberry sherbet, divided

Stir Hawaiian Punch, club soda, ginger ale, water and 2 cups sherbet in large punch bowl. Float remaining 2 cups sherbet in small scoops. *Makes about 18 cups*

Hot Chocolate

6 ounces semisweet chocolate, finely chopped
½ to ¾ cup sugar
1 quart (8 cups) milk, divided
2 teaspoons vanilla
Whipped cream or marshmallows (optional)

1. Combine chocolate, sugar and ½ cup milk in medium saucepan over medium-low heat. Cook, stirring constantly, until chocolate melts. Add remaining 7½ cups milk; heat until hot, stirring occasionally. *Do not boil.* Remove from heat; stir in vanilla. Keep hot in thermos.

2. Pour into mugs and top with whipped cream or marshmallows, if desired. Serve immediately. *Makes 8 cups*

Hot Cocoa: Substitute ½ cup unsweetened cocoa powder for semisweet chocolate and use 1 cup sugar; heat as directed.

Witches' Brew

2 quarts (8 cups) apple cider
½ cup honey
2 teaspoons ground cinnamon
½ teaspoon ground nutmeg
1 quart vanilla ice cream

Combine cider, honey, cinnamon and nutmeg in food processor or blender until smooth. Pour into cups or punch bowl; top with scoops of ice cream. Sprinkle with additional nutmeg. Serve immediately. *Makes 16 cups*

Serving Suggestion: Add a few drops of desired food coloring to ingredients in food processor to make a scary brew.

Lighten Up: To reduce fat, replace vanilla ice cream with reduced-fat or fat-free ice cream or frozen yogurt.

Prep Time: 10 minutes

Holiday Citrus Punch

Ingredients
> 1 **pint vanilla frozen yogurt, softened**
> **Fresh or frozen raspberries**
> 1 **can (12 ounces) frozen lemonade concentrate, thawed**
> 1 **can (12 ounces) frozen orange-cranberry juice concentrate, thawed**
> 1 **can (12 ounces) frozen Ruby Red grapefruit juice concentrate, thawed**
> 2 **cups cold water**
> ¼ **cup lime juice**
> 2 **bottles (28 ounces each) ginger ale, chilled**

Supplies
> **Parchment paper**
> **Assorted cookie cutters in star, snowflake or holiday shapes**

1. Line 9-inch square baking pan with parchment paper. Spread yogurt evenly into prepared pan; freeze until firm. Meanwhile, place baking sheet in freezer to chill.

2. Remove frozen yogurt from baking pan. Using cookie cutters, cut out desired shapes from frozen yogurt. Transfer cutouts to chilled baking sheet. Press raspberry into center of each yogurt cutout; freeze until ready to serve.

3. Combine fruit juice concentrates, water and lime juice in punch bowl. Just before serving, pour in ginger ale. Float yogurt cutouts in punch. *Makes about 13 cups*

 Save Time

> *If you don't have time to make the yogurt cutouts, add scoops of yogurt to the punch bowl or to each beverage cup for Holiday Citrus Float Punch.*

Chocolate Root Beer Float

- 1 tablespoon sugar
- 2 teaspoons HERSHEY'S Cocoa
- 1 tablespoon hot water
- 1 scoop vanilla ice cream
  Cold root beer

1. Stir together sugar and cocoa in 12-ounce glass; stir in water.

2. Add ice cream and enough root beer to half fill glass; stir gently. Fill glass with root beer. Stir; serve immediately.   *Makes 1½ cups*

Merry Mango Fizz

- 1 bottle (64 ounces) MAUNA LA'I® ¡Mango Mango!® Juice Drink
- 1 bottle (32 ounces) cranberry juice cocktail
- 1 bottle (32 ounces) ginger ale
- 2 cups vanilla ice cream
  Fresh or frozen strawberries, as needed

Combine Mauna La'i ¡Mango Mango! Juice Drink and cranberry juice cocktail in large punch bowl. Fifteen minutes before serving, add ginger ale and ice cream. Do not stir. Garnish with strawberries.

Makes 18 cups

Quick Apple Punch

- 4 cups MOTT'S® Apple Juice
- 2 cups cranberry juice cocktail
- 2 tablespoons lemon juice
- 1 liter ginger ale, chilled
  Crushed ice, as needed

In large bowl, combine apple juice, cranberry juice, and lemon juice. Fifteen minutes before serving, add ginger ale and crushed ice. Do not stir.   *Makes about 10 cups*

Crunchy
Snack Mixes

*Find endless combinations for snack mixes that kids are
sure to love. Fill decorated goodie bags or party cups
for easy-to-serve crunchy treats.*

Spicy, Fruity Popcorn Mix

4 cups lightly salted popcorn
2 cups corn cereal squares
1½ cups dried pineapple wedges
1 package (6 ounces) dried fruit bits
Butter-flavored nonstick cooking spray
2 tablespoons sugar
1 tablespoon ground cinnamon
1 cup yogurt-covered raisins

1. Preheat oven to 350°F. Combine popcorn, cereal, pineapple and
fruit bits in large bowl; mix lightly. Transfer to 15×10-inch jelly-roll
pan. Spray mixture generously with cooking spray.

2. Combine sugar and cinnamon in small bowl. Sprinkle ½ of the
sugar mixture over popcorn mixture; toss lightly to coat. Spray mixture
again with additional cooking spray. Add remaining sugar mixture;
mix lightly.

3. Bake snack mix 10 minutes, stirring after 5 minutes. Cool completely
in pan on wire rack. Add raisins; mix lightly.   *Makes 7 to 8 cups*

Cinnamon Trail Mix

2 cups corn cereal squares
2 cups whole wheat cereal squares or whole wheat
    cereal squares with mini graham crackers
1½ cups fat-free oyster crackers
½ cup broken sesame snack sticks
2 tablespoons margarine or butter, melted
1 teaspoon ground cinnamon
¼ teaspoon ground nutmeg
½ cup bite-size fruit-flavored candy pieces

1. Preheat oven to 350°F. Spray 13×9-inch baking pan with nonstick cooking spray.

2. Place cereals, oyster crackers and sesame sticks in prepared pan; mix lightly.

3. Combine margarine, cinnamon and nutmeg in small bowl; mix well. Drizzle evenly over cereal mixture; toss to coat.

4. Bake 12 to 14 minutes or until golden brown, stirring gently after 6 minutes. Cool completely. Stir in candies. *Makes 6 cups*

Critter Munch

1½ cups animal cracker cookies
½ (6-ounce) package cheddar or original flavor
    goldfish crackers (1½ cups)
1 cup dried tart cherries
1 cup candy-coated chocolate candy
1 cup honey roasted peanuts (optional)

1. Put animal crackers, goldfish crackers, dried cherries, candy and peanuts, if desired, in a large mixing bowl.

2. Carefully stir with a spoon.

3. Store in a tightly covered container at room temperature.
Makes 5 cups

Favorite recipe from **Cherry Marketing Institute**

Crunchy Cherry Party Mix

- 4 cups bite-size corn or rice square cereal
- 2 cups bite-size wheat square cereal
- 2 cups broken whole grain Melba toast
- 2 cups small fat-free pretzel twists
- 3 tablespoons margarine or butter, melted
- 1 tablespoon Worcestershire sauce
- 2 teaspoons chili powder
- ¼ teaspoon garlic powder
- ¼ teaspoon onion powder
- ⅛ teaspoon ground red pepper
- 1½ cups dried tart cherries

Put corn or rice cereal, wheat cereal, Melba toast and pretzels in a large bowl; stir to mix. In a measuring cup or small bowl, stir together melted margarine or butter, Worcestershire sauce, chili powder, garlic powder, onion powder and ground red pepper. Drizzle over cereal mixture. Toss to coat.

Spread cereal mixture in a 15×10×1-inch (or a 13×9×2-inch) baking pan. Bake in a preheated 300°F oven about 25 minutes, stirring every 7 to 8 minutes. Remove from oven; stir in dried cherries. Let cool completely. Store in a tightly covered container for up to 1 week.

Makes 20 (½-cup) servings

Favorite recipe from **Cherry Marketing Institute**

Make It Special

Snack mixes are terrific choices for classroom treats because they can be eaten without extra utensils and portioned in any size. Best of all, they are lifesavers from room moms because they can be easily prepared ahead of time.

Sweet Nothings Trail Mix

    5 cups rice and corn cereal squares
  1½ cups raisins
  1½ cups small thin pretzel sticks, broken into pieces
    1 cup candy-coated chocolate pieces
    1 cup peanuts (optional)

1. Have children decorate small resealable food storage bags with Valentine's Day or other holiday stickers, if desired.

2. Combine cereal, raisins, pretzels, chocolate pieces and peanuts, if desired, in large resealable plastic food storage bag; shake well. Distribute evenly among decorated bags or serve in large bowl.

Makes 10 cups

Party Favors: To serve this recipe as party favors, wrap handfuls of trail mix in colored plastic wrap and tie with festive ribbons.

Prep and Cook Time: 10 minutes

Double Peanut Snack Mix

    4 cups sweet shredded oat cereal
    1 cup peanuts
  ½ cup butter or margarine
  ½ cup JIF® Creamy Peanut Butter
    1 teaspoon ground cinnamon

Preheat oven to 350°F.

In a large bowl, combine cereal and peanuts.

In small saucepan heat butter or margarine, JIF® peanut butter and cinnamon over low heat until butter and JIF® are melted. Stir until blended.

Slowly pour over cereal mixture, mixing well. Spread into 13×9×2-inch baking pan. Bake 10 to 12 minutes; stir occasionally. Cool.

Makes 4 cups

Popcorn Crunchies

  12 **cups popped corn (about ¾ cup unpopped)**
1½ **cups sugar**
  ⅓ **cup water**
  ⅓ **cup corn syrup**
  2 **tablespoons butter or margarine**
  1 **teaspoon vanilla**

Preheat oven to 250°F. Grease large shallow roasting pan. Add popcorn. Keep warm in oven while making caramel mixture.

Place sugar, water and corn syrup in heavy 2-quart saucepan. Stir over low heat until sugar has dissolved and mixture comes to a boil. Carefully clip candy thermometer to side of pan (do not let bulb touch bottom of pan). Cook over low heat, without stirring, about 10 minutes or until thermometer registers 280°F. Occasionally wash down any sugar crystals that form on side of the pan using pastry brush dipped in warm water. Immediately remove from heat. Stir in butter and vanilla until smooth.

Pour hot syrup mixture slowly over warm popcorn, turning to coat kernels evenly. Set aside until cool enough to handle but warm enough to shape. Butter hands. Working quickly, lightly press warm mixture into 2-inch balls. Cool completely. Store in airtight container.

Makes about 14 popcorn balls

Make It Special

Popcorn Crunchies also make fabulous tree ornaments. Cool balls completely and wrap each ball with enough decorative plastic wrap to pull wrap together at the top. Secure with a ribbon which can be formed into a bow or a loop for hanging.

Cranberry-Orange Snack Mix

- **2 cups oatmeal cereal squares**
- **2 cups corn cereal squares**
- **2 cups mini pretzels**
- **1 cup whole almonds (optional)**
- **¼ cup butter**
- **⅓ cup frozen orange juice concentrate, thawed**
- **3 tablespoons packed brown sugar**
- **1 teaspoon ground cinnamon**
- **¾ teaspoon ground ginger**
- **¼ teaspoon ground nutmeg**
- **⅔ cup dried cranberries or raisins**

1. Preheat oven to 250°F. Spray 13×9-inch baking pan with nonstick cooking spray. Combine cereal squares, pretzels and almonds, if desired, in large bowl; set aside.

2. Melt butter in medium microwavable bowl at HIGH 45 to 60 seconds. Stir in orange juice concentrate, brown sugar, cinnamon, ginger and nutmeg until blended. Pour over cereal mixture; stir well to coat. Place in prepared pan and spread in single layer.

3. Bake 50 minutes, stirring every 10 minutes. Stir in cranberries. Let cool in pan on wire rack, leaving uncovered until mixture is crisp. Store in airtight container or resealable plastic food storage bags.

Makes 7 cups

Play It Safe

When planning classroom treats, keep in mind special dietary needs of the students. Snack mixes can easily be customized to meet most dietary needs without singling out any student. For example, if some students are allergic to peanuts, just leave them out of the mix.

Dirt Bites

- 4½ cups party mix or crispy multigrain cereal
- 2 tablespoons Butter Flavor CRISCO® Stick or Butter Flavor CRISCO® All-Vegetable Shortening
- ½ cup chocolate chips
- ¼ cup peanut butter
- ½ teaspoon vanilla
- ¾ cup powdered sugar

Measure party mix or cereal and set aside in large mixing bowl.

Melt Crisco® shortening, chocolate chips and peanut butter together in saucepan on low heat (or microwave on 50% power checking at 1 minute intervals).

Remove mixture from heat and stir in vanilla. Pour over cereal and mix until all coated.

Add powdered sugar to zipper bag; add coated cereal and toss to coat all.

Spread double coated cereal onto sheet of wax paper to cool. Transfer to clean zipper bag with slotted spoon. Discard excess sugar.

Makes 4½ cups

Peanut Butter 'n' Chocolate Chips Snack Mix

- 6 cups bite-size crisp corn, rice or wheat squares cereal
- 3 cups miniature pretzels
- 2 cups toasted oat cereal rings
- 1 cup raisins or dried fruit bits
- 1 cup HERSHEY'S Semi-Sweet Chocolate Chips
- 1 cup REESE'S® Peanut Butter Chips

Stir together all ingredients in large bowl. Store in airtight container at room temperature.

Makes 14 cups

Pleasin' Peanutty Snack Mix

4 cups whole wheat cereal squares *or* 2 cups whole wheat and
    2 cups corn or rice cereal squares
2 cups small pretzel twists or goldfish-shaped pretzels
½ cup dry-roasted peanuts
2 tablespoons creamy peanut butter
1 tablespoon honey
1 tablespoon apple juice or water
2 teaspoons vanilla
    Butter-flavored nonstick cooking spray
½ cup raisins, dried fruit bits or dried cherries (optional)

1. Preheat oven to 250°F.

2. Combine cereal, pretzels and peanuts in large bowl; set aside.

3. Combine peanut butter, honey and apple juice in small microwavable bowl. Microwave at HIGH 30 seconds or until hot. Stir in vanilla.

4. Drizzle peanut butter mixture evenly over cereal mixture; toss lightly to evenly coat. Place mixture in single layer in ungreased 15×10-inch jelly-roll pan; coat lightly with cooking spray.

5. Bake 8 minutes; stir. Continue baking 8 to 9 minutes or until golden brown. Remove from oven. Add raisins, if desired; mix lightly.

6. Spread mixture in single layer on large sheet of foil to cool.

Makes 6 cups

Make It Special

Add excitement to the party by using empty ice cream cones as individual edible serving bowls for serving snack mixes. Look for colored cones to add extra pizazz.

Brontosaurus Bites

        4 cups air-popped popcorn
        2 cups mini-dinosaur grahams
        2 cups corn cereal squares
    1½ cups dried pineapple wedges
        1 package (6 ounces) dried fruit bits
            Butter-flavored nonstick cooking spray
        1 tablespoon plus 1½ teaspoons sugar
    1½ teaspoons ground cinnamon
        ½ teaspoon ground nutmeg
        1 cup yogurt-covered raisins

1. Preheat oven to 350°F. Combine popcorn, grahams, cereal, pineapple and fruit bits in large bowl; mix lightly. Transfer to 15×10-inch jelly-roll pan. Spray mixture generously with cooking spray.

2. Combine sugar, cinnamon and nutmeg in small bowl. Sprinkle ½ of the sugar mixture over popcorn mixture; toss lightly to coat. Spray mixture again with additional cooking spray. Add remaining sugar mixture; mix lightly.

3. Bake snack mix 10 minutes, stirring after 5 minutes. Cool completely in pan on wire rack. Add raisins; mix lightly.   *Makes about 9 cups*

Gorilla Grub: Substitute plain raisins for the yogurt-covered raisins and ¼ cup grated Parmesan cheese for the sugar, cinnamon and nutmeg.

Make It Special

Kids may want to bring snacks home. Pick up small sturdy paper plates, clear plastic bags and assorted colorful ribbons. Or, prepare take-home treats ahead of time. Wrap extra snack mix in festive colored paper napkins, party bags or small plastic food storage bags decorated with stickers.

Sticks 'n' Stones

> **4 cups** caramel corn
> **4 cups** unseasoned croutons
> **¾ cup** sesame sticks
> **¾ cup** honey roasted peanuts (optional)
> **¾ cup** toasted pumpkin or sunflower seeds*
> **¼ cup** (½ stick) butter, melted
> **1 package** (1 ounce) dry ranch-style salad dressing mix
> **10** flat-bottomed ice cream cones

To toast seeds, place in single layer on baking sheet. Bake at 350°F for 7 to 10 minutes or until golden brown, stirring occasionally. Cool completely.

1. Preheat oven to 300°F.

2. Combine caramel corn, croutons, sesame sticks, peanuts, if desired, and toasted pumpkin seeds on ungreased jelly-roll pan. Drizzle with butter; sprinkle with dressing mix and toss to coat.

3. Bake 15 minutes, stirring occasionally. Cool 10 minutes on pan. Turn out onto paper towels; cool completely.

4. Tie cones with ribbons, if desired. Serve snack mix in cones.

Makes 10 cups

Original Ranch® Snack Mix

> **8 cups** KELLOGG'S® CRISPIX®* cereal
> **2½ cups** small pretzels
> **2½ cups** bite-size Cheddar cheese crackers (optional)
> **3 tablespoons** vegetable oil
> **1 packet** (1 ounce) HIDDEN VALLEY® The Original Ranch®
>   Salad Dressing & Seasoning Mix

Kellogg's® and Crispix® are registered trademarks of Kellogg Company.

Combine cereal, pretzels and crackers in a gallon-size Glad® Zipper Storage Bag. Pour oil over mixture. Seal bag and toss to coat. Add salad dressing & seasoning mix; seal bag and toss again until coated.

Makes 10 cups

Chocolate & Fruit Snack Mix

- ½ cup (1 stick) butter or margarine
- 2 tablespoons sugar
- 1 tablespoon HERSHEY'S Cocoa or HERSHEY'S Dutch Processed Cocoa
- ½ teaspoon ground cinnamon
- 3 cups bite-size crisp rice squares cereal
- 3 cups bite-size crisp wheat squares cereal
- 2 cups toasted oat cereal rings
- 1 cup cashews
- 1½ cups (6-ounce package) dried fruit bits
- 1 cup HERSHEY'S Semi-Sweet Chocolate Chips

1. Place butter in 4-quart microwave-safe bowl. Microwave at HIGH (100%) 1 minute or until melted; stir in sugar, cocoa and cinnamon. Add cereals and cashews; stir until evenly coated. Microwave at HIGH 3 minutes, stirring after each minute; stir in dried fruit. Microwave at HIGH 3 minutes, stirring after each minute.

2. Cool completely; stir in chocolate chips. Store in tightly covered container in cool, dry place.   *Makes about 11 cups*

Patchwork Pop Corn Party Mix

- 3 quarts popped JOLLY TIME® Pop Corn
- 2 cups rice or wheat cereal squares
- ½ cup dried cranberries or dried tart cherries
- 1 cup coarsely chopped walnuts, toasted
- 3 tablespoons butter or margarine
- ½ teaspoon maple extract

Place popped pop corn, cereal, cranberries and walnuts in large bowl. Melt butter in small pan. Stir in maple extract. Pour over pop corn mixture; toss well.   *Makes about 14 cups*

Holiday Party Mix

 9 cups oven-toasted corn cereal squares
 4 cups popped popcorn
 1½ cups dry-roasted peanuts
 1 cup packed light brown sugar
 ½ cup (1 stick) butter or margarine
 ½ cup light corn syrup
 1 teaspoon vanilla extract
 ½ teaspoon baking soda
 1¾ cups (10-ounce package) NESTLÉ® TOLL HOUSE® Holiday
    Shapes & Morsels
 1 package (7.5 ounces) white fudge-covered pretzels

PREHEAT oven to 250°F. Grease large roasting pan.

MIX cereal, popped popcorn and peanuts in large bowl. Pour into prepared pan.

COMBINE brown sugar, butter and corn syrup in medium, *heavy-duty* saucepan. Bring to a boil over medium heat, stirring constantly. Boil, without stirring, for 5 minutes. Remove from heat; stir in vanilla extract and baking soda. Pour evenly over cereal mixture; stir to coat evenly.

BAKE for 45 minutes, stirring every 15 minutes. Cool completely in pan, stirring frequently to break apart mixture. Stir in Shapes & Morsels and pretzels. Store in airtight container.   *Makes about 20 cups*

Make It Special

Be sure to take advantage of seasonally decorated, shaped or colored food items like morsels and pretzels. These special holiday items make it easy to add that extra touch to holiday treats.

Teddy Bear Party Mix

- 4 cups crisp cinnamon graham cereal
- 2 cups honey flavored teddy-shaped graham snacks
- 1 can (1½ ounces) *French's®* Potato Sticks
- 3 tablespoons melted unsalted butter
- 2 tablespoons *French's®* Worcestershire Sauce
- 1 tablespoon packed brown sugar
- ¼ teaspoon ground cinnamon
- 1 cup sweetened dried cranberries or raisins
- ½ cup chocolate, peanut butter or carob chips

1. Preheat oven to 350°F. Lightly spray jelly-roll pan with nonstick cooking spray. Combine cereal, graham snacks and potato sticks in large bowl.

2. Combine butter, Worcestershire, sugar and cinnamon in small bowl; toss with cereal mixture. Transfer to prepared pan. Bake 12 minutes. Cool completely.

3. Stir in dried cranberries and chips. Store in an air-tight container.

Makes about 7 cups

Prep Time: 5 minutes • Cook Time: 12 minutes

Cereal Trail Mix

- ¼ cup (½ stick) butter or margarine
- 2 tablespoons sugar
- 1 teaspoon ground cinnamon
- 1 cup bite-size oat cereal squares
- 1 cup bite-size wheat cereal squares
- 1 cup bite-size rice cereal squares
- ¼ cup toasted slivered almonds
- ¾ cup raisins

Melt butter at HIGH 1½ minutes in large microwave-safe bowl. Add sugar and cinnamon; mix well. Add cereals and nuts; stir to coat. Microwave at HIGH 2 minutes. Stir well. Microwave 2 minutes more; stir well. Add raisins. Microwave an additional 2 to 3 minutes, stirring well after 2 minutes. Spread on paper towels; mix will become crisp as it cools. Store tightly covered.

Makes about 4 cups

Monster Munch

6 squares (2 ounces each) almond bark, divided
1½ cups pretzel sticks
    Orange food coloring
2 cups graham cereal
¾ cup Halloween colored candy-coated chocolate pieces
¾ cup miniature marshmallows
½ cup chocolate sprinkles

1. Place 1½ squares almond bark in small microwavable bowl. Microwave at MEDIUM (50% power) 1 minute; stir. Repeat steps as necessary, stirring at 15-second intervals, until completely melted.

2. Place pretzel sticks in large bowl. Add melted almond bark and stir until all pieces are coated. Spread coated pretzel sticks out on waxed paper, separating individual pieces; let set.

3. Place remaining 4½ squares almond bark in medium microwavable bowl. Microwave at MEDIUM (50% power) 1 minute; stir. Repeat steps as necessary, stirring at 15-second intervals, until completely melted. Stir in food coloring until almond bark is bright orange.

4. Place cereal in large bowl. Add half of orange-colored almond bark and stir until cereal is evenly coated. Add chocolate pieces, marshmallows and remaining almond bark; stir until mix is evenly coated. Stir in pretzel sticks. Break mix into small clusters and spread out on waxed paper. Sprinkle clusters with chocolate sprinkles; let set.

Makes about 5 cups

 Make It Special

To make a signature class snack mix, ask each student to bring their favorite cereal, crackers or dried fruit. Combine all the ingredients in a huge container or popcorn tin. Shake and serve. And, don't forget to give the mix a special name.

"M&M's"® Family Party Mix

  2 tablespoons butter or margarine*
  ¼ cup honey*
  2 cups favorite grain cereal *or* 3 cups granola
  1 cup coarsely chopped nuts
  1 cup thin pretzel pieces
  1 cup raisins
  2 cups "M&M's"® Chocolate Mini Baking Bits

For a drier mix, eliminate butter and honey. Simply combine dry ingredients and do not bake.

Preheat oven to 300°F. In large saucepan over low heat, melt butter; add honey until well blended. Remove from heat; add cereal, nuts, pretzel pieces and raisins, stirring until all pieces are evenly coated. Spread mixture onto ungreased cookie sheet. Bake about 10 minutes. Do not overbake. Spread mixture onto waxed paper; cool completely. In large bowl combine mixture and "M&M's"® Chocolate Mini Baking Bits. Store in tightly covered container.   *Makes about 6 cups*

Caramel Corn

  ½ cup packed brown sugar
  ⅓ cup light corn syrup
  ¼ Butter Flavor CRISCO® Stick or ¼ cup Butter Flavor CRISCO®
      All-Vegetable Shortening
  ½ teaspoon vanilla
  2 quarts popped popcorn
  1 cup coarsely chopped blanched almonds (optional)

Preheat oven to 300°F. Generously grease baking sheet.

In Dutch oven blend brown sugar, corn syrup, Butter Flavor CRISCO® and vanilla. Cook over medium-high heat for about 2 minutes, or until light and foamy, stirring constantly. Remove from heat. Add popcorn, tossing to coat. Stir in almonds, if desired. Spread on prepared baking sheet.

Bake at 300°F for 15 minutes, stirring once. Cool. Break into bite-size pieces. Store in covered container.   *Makes 8 cups*

Birthday Parties

Make birthdays extra special with attractively decorated treats.
Colorful homemade cookies, cakes or cupcakes
make any party memorable.

Dipped, Drizzled & Decorated Pretzels

- 1 bag chocolate or flavored chips (choose semisweet, bittersweet, milk chocolate, green mint, white chocolate, butterscotch, peanut butter or a combination)
- 1 bag pretzel rods
- Assorted toppings: jimmies, sprinkles, chopped nuts, coconut, toasted coconut, cookie crumbs, colored sugars

Microwave Directions

1. Place chips in microwavable bowl. (Be sure bowl and utensils are completely dry.) Cover with plastic wrap and turn back one corner to vent. Microwave at HIGH for 1 minute; stir. Return to microwave and continue cooking in 30-second intervals until chips are completely melted. Check and stir frequently.

2. Dip one half of each pretzel rod into melted chocolate and decorate. Roll coated end of several pretzels in toppings. Drizzle others with contrasting color/flavor melted chips. (Drizzle melted chocolate out of spoon while rotating pretzel, to get even coverage.)

3. Place decorated pretzels on cooling rack; set over baking sheet lined with waxed-paper. Let coating harden completely. Do not refrigerate.

Makes about 24 pretzels

Cookies & Cream Cupcakes

2¼ cups all-purpose flour
1 tablespoon baking powder
½ teaspoon salt
1⅔ cups sugar
1 cup milk
½ cup (1 stick) butter, softened
2 teaspoons vanilla
3 egg whites
1 cup crushed chocolate sandwich cookies (about 10 cookies) plus additional for garnish
1 container (16 ounces) vanilla frosting

1. Preheat oven to 350°F. Line 24 regular-size (2½-inch) muffin pan cups with paper baking cups.

2. Sift flour, baking powder and salt together in large bowl. Stir in sugar. Add milk, butter and vanilla; beat with electric mixer at low speed 30 seconds. Beat at medium speed 2 minutes. Add egg whites; beat 2 minutes. Stir in 1 cup crushed cookies.

3. Spoon batter into prepared muffin cups. Bake 20 to 25 minutes or until toothpicks inserted into centers come out clean. Cool in pans on wire racks 10 minutes. Remove to racks; cool completely.

4. Frost cupcakes; garnish with additional crushed cookies.

Makes 24 cupcakes

Make It Special

Tempt small appetites with miniature-size instead of regular-size cupcakes. Children and moms will enjoy these bite-size goodies that are tasty, colorful, fun and less messy to eat.

Fruit and Nut Bars

  1 cup unsifted all-purpose flour
  1 cup uncooked quick oats
  ⅔ cup brown sugar
  2 teaspoons baking soda
  ½ teaspoon salt
  ½ teaspoon ground cinnamon
  ⅔ cup buttermilk
  3 tablespoons vegetable oil
  2 egg whites, lightly beaten
  1 Washington Golden Delicious apple, cored and chopped
  ½ cup dried cranberries or raisins, chopped
  ¼ cup chopped nuts
  2 tablespoons flaked coconut (optional)

1. Heat oven to 375°F. Lightly grease 9-inch square baking pan. In large mixing bowl, combine flour, oats, brown sugar, baking soda, salt and cinnamon; stir to blend.

2. Add buttermilk, oil and egg whites; beat with electric mixer just until mixed. Stir in apple, dried fruit and nuts; spread evenly in pan and top with coconut, if desired. Bake 20 to 25 minutes or until cake tester inserted in center comes out clean. Cool and cut into 16 bars.

Makes 16 bars

Favorite recipe from **Washington Apple Commission**

Make It Special

Bar cookies are a fantastic solution for classroom treats with less sugar. Moist and delicious, many fabulous tasting bar cookies eliminate sugary frostings but include nutritious oats and dried fruits.

Smiley Oatmeal Cookies

Cookies

   1 **Butter Flavor CRISCO® Stick or 1 cup Butter Flavor CRISCO® All-Vegetable Shortening**

   1 **cup firmly packed light brown sugar**

   ¾ **cup granulated sugar**

   2 **eggs**

   1 **teaspoon vanilla**

 2½ **cups all-purpose flour**

   1 **teaspoon baking soda**

   ½ **teaspoon salt**

   1 **cup oats (quick or old-fashioned, uncooked)**

   1 **cup flaked coconut**

Frosting

   2 **cups confectioners' sugar**

   ¼ **Butter Flavor CRISCO® Stick or ¼ cup Butter Flavor CRISCO® All-Vegetable Shortening**

   5 **to 6 teaspoons milk**

Decoration

     Peanut butter candy pieces

     Red licorice laces

1. Heat oven to 350°F. Place sheets of foil on countertop for cooling cookies.

2. For cookies, combine 1 cup shortening, brown sugar, granulated sugar, eggs and vanilla in large bowl. Beat at medium speed of electric mixer until well blended.

3. Combine flour, baking soda and salt. Add gradually to creamed mixture at low speed. Beat until well blended. Stir in oats and coconut with spoon. Shape tablespoonfuls of dough into 1-inch balls. Place 2 inches apart on ungreased baking sheet.

4. Bake at 350°F for 8 to 10 minutes or until very light brown and set. *Do not overbake.* Flatten slightly with spatula to level tops. Cool 2 minutes on baking sheet. Remove cookies to foil to cool completely.

continued on page 48

Smiley Oatmeal Cookies, continued

5. For frosting, combine confectioners' sugar, ¼ cup shortening and 5 teaspoons milk in medium bowl. Beat at low speed until well blended and creamy, adding additional 1 teaspoon milk if needed. Spread thin layer on cookies. Decorate before frosting sets.

6. For decoration, make faces on cookies by placing candy pieces for eyes. Cut licorice into short strips. Form into different shapes for mouths. Press into frosting.   *Makes about 60 cookies*

Haystacks

   ¼ **Butter Flavor CRISCO® Stick or ¼ cup Butter Flavor CRISCO® All-Vegetable Shortening**
   ½ **cup JIF® Creamy Peanut Butter**
   2 **cups butterscotch chips**
   6 **cups corn flakes**
   ⅔ **cup miniature semisweet chocolate chips**
      Chopped peanuts or chocolate jimmies (optional)

Combine ¼ cup shortening, JIF® peanut butter and butterscotch chips in large microwave-safe bowl. Cover with waxed paper. Microwave 1 minute at MEDIUM (50% power); stir. Repeat until smooth (or melt on rangetop in small saucepan on very low heat, stirring constantly).

Pour corn flakes into large bowl. Pour hot butterscotch mixture over flakes. Stir with spoon until flakes are coated. Stir in chocolate chips.

Spoon ½ cup mixture into mounds on waxed paper-lined baking sheets. Sprinkle with chopped nuts, if desired. Refrigerate until firm.
Makes 36 cookies

Peanut Butter Crispy Treats

- 6 tablespoons butter or margarine
- 2 (10-ounce) packages marshmallows
- 2 cups JIF® Creamy Peanut Butter
- 10 cups crisp rice cereal
    - CRISCO® No-Stick Cooking Spray
- 2½ cups sifted powdered sugar

GLAZE (optional)
- ½ cup butter or margarine
- ½ cup brown sugar, packed
- 2 tablespoons milk
- 1 teaspoon vanilla

In large saucepan, melt butter over low heat. Add marshmallows. Stir until completely melted and remove from heat.

Stir in JIF® and mix well to incorporate. Add cereal and stir until well coated.

Press into two 9-inch pans, well coated with CRISCO® No-Stick Cooking Spray, and allow to cool.

Combine all ingredients for glaze in a small saucepan. Cook for 2 minutes over medium heat or until sugar dissolves. Pour glaze over top of bars and allow to cool before cutting and serving.

Makes 32 bars

⋊ Make It Special

Do not store Peanut Butter Crispy Treats in refrigerator. The moisture will cause the cereal to lose crispness. Individually wrap bars in plastic wrap for ready-to-serve treats. Store in a cool dry place.

Banana Split Cupcakes

   1 package (about 18 ounces) yellow cake mix, divided
   1 cup water
   1 cup mashed ripe bananas
   3 eggs
   1 cup chopped drained maraschino cherries
1½ cups miniature semisweet chocolate chips, divided
1½ cups prepared vanilla frosting
   1 cup marshmallow creme
   1 teaspoon shortening
 30 whole maraschino cherries, drained and patted dry

1. Preheat oven to 350°F. Line 30 regular-size (2½-inch) muffin cups with paper baking cups.

2. Reserve 2 tablespoons cake mix. Combine remaining cake mix, water, bananas and eggs in large bowl. Beat at low speed of electric mixer until moistened, about 30 seconds. Beat at medium speed 2 minutes. Combine chopped cherries and reserved cake mix in small bowl. Stir chopped cherry mixture and 1 cup chocolate chips into batter.

3. Spoon batter into prepared muffin cups. Bake 15 to 20 minutes or until toothpicks inserted into centers come out clean. Cool in pans on wire racks 10 minutes. Remove to wire racks; cool completely.

4. Combine frosting and marshmallow creme in medium bowl until well blended. Frost cupcakes.

5. Combine remaining ½ cup chocolate chips and shortening in small microwavable bowl. Microwave at HIGH 30 to 45 seconds, stirring after 30 seconds, or until smooth. Drizzle chocolate mixture over cupcakes. Place one whole cherry on each cupcake.

Makes 30 cupcakes

Note: If desired, omit chocolate drizzle and top cupcakes with colored sprinkles.

Chocolate Marbled Blondies

½ cup (1 stick) butter or margarine, softened
½ cup firmly packed light brown sugar
1 large egg
2 teaspoons vanilla extract
1½ cups all-purpose flour
1¼ teaspoons baking soda
1 cup "M&M's"® Chocolate Mini Baking Bits, divided
4 ounces cream cheese, softened
2 tablespoons granulated sugar
1 large egg yolk
¼ cup unsweetened cocoa powder

Preheat oven to 350°F. Lightly grease 9×9×2-inch baking pan; set aside. In large bowl cream butter and brown sugar until light and fluffy; beat in egg and vanilla. In medium bowl combine flour and baking soda; blend into creamed mixture. Stir in ⅔ cup "M&M's"® Chocolate Mini Baking Bits; set aside. Dough will be stiff. In separate bowl beat together cream cheese, granulated sugar and egg yolk until smooth; stir in cocoa powder until well blended. Place chocolate-cheese mixture in six equal portions evenly onto bottom of prepared pan. Place reserved dough around cheese mixture and swirl slightly with tines of fork. Pat down evenly on top. Sprinkle with remaining ⅓ cup "M&M's"® Chocolate Mini Baking Bits. Bake 25 to 30 minutes or until toothpick inserted in center comes out with moist crumbs. Cool completely. Cut into bars. Store in refrigerator in tightly covered container. *Makes 16 bars*

Make It Special

Bring out the creative baker in you with easy-to-make bar cookies. Dazzle cookie monsters with creative cookie treats decorated with brightly colored bits.

Reese's® Haystacks

1⅔ cups (10-ounce package) REESE'S® Peanut Butter Chips
1 tablespoon shortening (do *not* use butter, margarine, spread or oil)
2½ cups (5-ounce can) chow mein noodles

1. Line tray with wax paper.

2. Place peanut butter chips and shortening in medium microwave-safe bowl. Microwave at HIGH (100%) 1 minute; stir. If necessary, microwave at HIGH an additional 15 seconds at a time, stirring after each heating, just until chips are melted and mixture is smooth when stirred. Immediately add chow mein noodles; stir to coat.

3. Drop mixture by heaping teaspoons onto prepared tray or into paper candy cups. Let stand until firm. If necessary, cover and refrigerate several minutes until firm. Store in tightly covered container.

Makes about 24 treats

Polar Bear Banana Bites

1 medium banana, cut into 6 equal-size pieces
¼ cup creamy peanut butter*
3 tablespoons fat-free (skim) milk
¼ cup miniature-size marshmallows
2 tablespoons unsalted dry-roasted peanuts, chopped (optional)
1 tablespoon chocolate-flavored decorator sprinkles

Soy butter or almond butter can be used in place of peanut butter.

1. Insert toothpick into each banana piece. Place on tray lined with waxed paper.

2. Whisk together peanut butter and milk. Combine marshmallows, peanuts, if desired, and chocolate sprinkles in shallow dish. Dip each banana piece in peanut butter mixture, draining off excess. Roll in marshmallow mixture. Place on tray; let stand until set.

Makes 6 pieces

Cookie Sundae Cups

1 package (18 ounces) refrigerated chocolate chip cookie dough
6 cups ice cream, any flavor
1¼ cups ice cream topping, any flavor
Can aerosol whipped cream
Colored sprinkles

1. Preheat oven to 350°F. Lightly grease 18 standard (2½-inch) muffin pan cups.

2. Remove dough from wrapper. Shape dough into 18 balls; press onto bottoms and up sides of prepared muffin cups.

3. Bake 14 to 18 minutes or until golden brown. Cool in muffin cups 10 minutes. Remove to wire rack; cool completely.

4. Place ⅓ cup ice cream in each cookie cup. Drizzle with ice cream topping. Top with whipped cream and colored sprinkles.

Makes 18 desserts

Note: Freeze ice cream in cookie cups until ready to serve. Add topping, whipped cream and sprinkles in the classroom.

Monkey's Uncle Sundae

Vanilla ice cream
Half of 1 banana, peeled and sliced
HERSHEY'S Chocolate Shell Topping
REDDI-WIP® Whipped Topping

● Place scoop of ice cream in shallow dessert dish.

● Place banana slices all around ice cream.

● Shake HERSHEY'S Chocolate Shell Topping according to instructions. Squeeze generous amount over ice cream. Allow to harden for 30 seconds.

● Top with liberal amount of REDDI-WIP Whipped Topping.

Makes 1 sundae

Chocolate Zucchini Snack Cake

1⅔ cups granulated sugar
½ cup (1 stick) butter, softened
½ cup vegetable oil
2 eggs
1½ teaspoons vanilla
2½ cups all-purpose flour
⅓ cup unsweetened cocoa powder
1 teaspoon baking soda
½ teaspoon salt
½ cup buttermilk
2 cups shredded zucchini
¾ cup chopped pecans (optional)
1 cup semisweet chocolate chips

1. Preheat oven to 325°F. Grease and flour 13×9-inch baking pan.

2. Beat sugar, butter and oil in large bowl with electric mixer at medium speed until well blended.

3. Add eggs, one at a time, beating well after each addition. Blend in vanilla.

4. Combine flour, cocoa, baking soda and salt in medium bowl. Add to butter mixture alternately with buttermilk, beating well after each addition. Stir in zucchini.

5. Pour into prepared pan. Sprinkle with pecans, if desired, and chocolate chips.

6. Bake 55 minutes or until toothpick inserted in center comes out clean; cool on wire rack. Cut into squares.   *Makes 24 squares*

Double Malted Cupcakes

Cupcakes
- 2 cups all-purpose flour
- ¼ cup malted milk powder
- 2 teaspoons baking powder
- ¼ teaspoon salt
- 1¾ cups granulated sugar
- ½ cup (1 stick) butter, softened
- 1 cup reduced-fat (2%) or whole milk
- 1½ teaspoons vanilla
- 3 egg whites

Frosting
- 4 ounces milk chocolate candy bar, broken into chunks
- ¼ cup (½ stick) butter
- ¼ cup whipping cream
- 1 tablespoon malted milk powder
- 1 teaspoon vanilla
- 1¾ cups powdered sugar
- 30 chocolate-covered malt ball candies

1. Preheat oven to 350°F. Line 30 regular-size (2½-inch) muffin cups with paper baking cups.

2. For cupcakes, combine flour, ¼ cup malted milk powder, baking powder and salt; mix well and set aside. Beat sugar and ½ cup butter with electric mixer at medium speed 1 minute. Add milk and 1½ teaspoons vanilla. Beat at low speed 30 seconds. Gradually beat in flour mixture; beat at medium speed 2 minutes. Add egg whites; beat 1 minute.

3. Spoon batter into prepared muffin cups filling ⅔ full. Bake 20 minutes or until golden brown and toothpicks inserted into centers come out clean. Cool in pans on wire racks 10 minutes. (Centers of cupcakes will sink slightly upon cooling.) Remove cupcakes to racks; cool completely. (At this point, cupcakes may be frozen up to 3 months.)

continued on page 62

4. For frosting, melt chocolate and ¼ cup butter in heavy medium saucepan over low heat, stirring frequently. Stir in cream, 1 tablespoon malted milk powder and 1 teaspoon vanilla; mix well. Gradually stir in powdered sugar. Cook 4 to 5 minutes, stirring constantly, until small lumps disappear. Remove from heat. Refrigerate 20 minutes, beating every 5 minutes or until frosting is spreadable.

5. Spread cooled cupcakes with frosting; decorate with chocolate-covered malt ball candies. Store at room temperature up to 24 hours or cover and refrigerate for up to 3 days before serving.

Makes 30 cupcakes

Monkey Bars

3 cups miniature marshmallows
½ cup honey
⅓ cup butter
¼ cup peanut butter
2 teaspoons vanilla
¼ teaspoon salt
4 cups crispy rice cereal
2 cups rolled oats, uncooked
½ cup flaked coconut
¼ cup peanuts

Combine marshmallows, honey, butter, peanut butter, vanilla and salt in medium saucepan. Melt marshmallow mixture over low heat, stirring constantly. Combine rice cereal, oats, coconut and peanuts in 13×9×2-inch baking pan. Pour marshmallow mixture over dry ingredients. Mix until thoroughly coated. Press mixture firmly into pan. Cool completely before cutting.

Makes 24 bars

Microwave Directions: Microwave marshmallows, honey, butter, peanut butter, vanilla and salt in 2-quart microwave-safe bowl on HIGH 2½ to 3 minutes. Continue as above.

Favorite recipe from **National Honey Board**

Mini Turtle Cupcakes

    1 **package (21.5 ounces) brownie mix plus ingredients
       to prepare mix**
  ½ **cup chopped pecans (optional)**
    1 **cup prepared or homemade dark chocolate frosting**
  ½ **cup coarsely chopped pecans, toasted (optional)**
  12 **caramels**
    1 **to 2 tablespoons whipping cream**

1. Heat oven to 350°F. Line 54 mini (1½-inch) muffin cups with paper baking cups.

2. Prepare brownie batter as directed on package. Stir in chopped pecans, if desired.

3. Spoon batter into prepared muffin cups filling ⅔ full. Bake 18 minutes or until toothpicks inserted into centers come out clean. Cool in pans on wire racks 5 minutes. Remove cupcakes to racks; cool completely. (At this point, cupcakes may be frozen up to 3 months. Thaw at room temperature before frosting.)

4. Spread frosting over cooled cupcakes; top with toasted pecans, if desired.

5. Combine caramels and 1 tablespoon cream in small saucepan. Cook and stir over low heat until caramels are melted and mixture is smooth. Add additional 1 tablespoon cream if needed. Spoon caramel decoratively over cupcakes. Store at room temperature up to 24 hours or cover and refrigerate for up to 3 days before serving.

Makes 54 mini cupcakes

Mini Pizza Cookies

1 20-ounce tube refrigerated sugar cookie dough
2 cups (16 ounces) prepared pink frosting
  "M&M's"® Chocolate Mini Baking Bits
  Variety of additional toppings such as shredded coconut,
    granola, raisins, nuts, small pretzels, snack mixes, sunflower
    seeds, popped corn and mini marshmallows

Preheat oven to 350°F. Lightly grease cookie sheets; set aside. Divide dough into 8 equal portions. On lightly floured surface, roll each portion of dough into ¼-inch-thick circle; place circles about 2 inches apart onto prepared cookie sheets. Bake 10 to 13 minutes or until golden brown on edges. Cool completely on wire racks. Spread top of each pizza with frosting; sprinkle with "M&M's"® Chocolate Mini Baking Bits and 2 or 3 suggested toppings. *Makes 8 large cookies*

Summer Fruits with Peanut Butter-Honey Dip

⅓ cup smooth or chunky peanut butter
2 tablespoons milk
2 tablespoons honey
1 tablespoon apple juice or water
⅛ teaspoon ground cinnamon
2 cups melon balls, including cantaloupe and honeydew
1 peach or nectarine, pitted and cut into 8 wedges
1 banana, peeled and thickly sliced

1. Place peanut butter in small bowl; gradually stir in milk and honey until blended. Stir in apple juice and cinnamon until mixture is smooth.

2. Serve dip along with prepared fruits.
Makes 4 servings (about ½ cup dip)

Prep Time: 20 minutes

Ultimate Rocky Road Cups

¾ **cup (1½ sticks) butter or margarine**
4 **squares (1 ounce each) unsweetened baking chocolate**
1½ **cups granulated sugar**
3 **large eggs**
1 **cup all-purpose flour**
1¾ **cups "M&M's"® Chocolate Mini Baking Bits**
¾ **cup coarsely chopped peanuts (optional)**
1 **cup mini marshmallows**

Preheat oven to 350°F. Generously grease 24 (2½-inch) muffin cups or line with foil liners. Place butter and chocolate in large microwave-safe bowl. Microwave on HIGH 1 minute; stir. Microwave on HIGH an additional 30 seconds; stir until chocolate is completely melted. Add sugar and eggs, one at a time, beating well after each addition; blend in flour. In separate bowl combine "M&M's"® Chocolate Mini Baking Bits and nuts, if desired; stir 1 cup baking bits mixture into brownie batter. Divide batter evenly among prepared muffin cups. Bake 20 minutes. Combine remaining baking bits mixture with marshmallows; divide evenly among muffin cups, topping hot brownies. Return to oven; bake 5 minutes longer. Cool completely before removing from muffin cups. Store in tightly covered container. *Makes 24 cups*

Mini Ultimate Rocky Road Cups: Prepare recipe as directed, dividing batter among 60 generously greased 2-inch mini muffin cups. Bake 15 minutes. Sprinkle with topping mixture; bake 5 minutes longer. Cool completely before removing from cups. Store in tightly covered container. Makes about 60 mini cups.

Ultimate Rocky Road Squares: Prepare recipe as directed, spreading batter into generously greased 13×9×2-inch baking pan. Bake 30 minutes. Sprinkle with topping mixture; bake 5 minutes longer. Cool completely. Cut into squares. Store in tightly covered container. Makes 24 squares.

Red's Rockin' Rainbow Cupcakes

2¼ cups all-purpose flour
1 tablespoon baking powder
½ teaspoon salt
1⅔ cups granulated sugar
½ cup (1 stick) butter, softened
1 cup milk
2 teaspoons vanilla extract
3 large egg whites
  Blue and assorted food colorings
1 container (16 ounces) white frosting
1½ cups "M&M's"® Chocolate Mini Baking Bits, divided

Preheat oven to 350°F. Lightly grease 24 (2¾-inch) muffin cups or line with paper or foil liners; set aside. In large bowl combine flour, baking powder and salt. Blend in sugar, butter, milk and vanilla; beat about 2 minutes. Add egg whites; beat 2 minutes. Divide batter evenly among prepared muffin cups. Place 2 drops desired food coloring into each muffin cup. Swirl gently with knife. Sprinkle evenly with ¾ cup "M&M's"® Chocolate Mini Baking Bits. Bake 20 to 25 minutes or until toothpick inserted in centers comes out clean. Cool completely on wire racks. Combine frosting and blue food coloring. Spread frosting over cupcakes; decorate with remaining ¾ cup "M&M's"® Chocolate Mini Baking Bits to make rainbows. Store in tightly covered container.

Makes 24 cupcakes

Tasty Teaching Tip

Make learning fun by letting kids decorate a cupcake or cookie with tubes of frosting, colorful candies or any edible decoration. Decorating activities can be fantastic opportunities for learning colors and numbers.

Inside-Out Peanut Butter Cookie Sandwiches

1¼ cups all-purpose flour
½ teaspoon baking soda
½ teaspoon salt
¾ cup (1½ sticks) butter, softened
⅔ cup creamy or chunky peanut butter
½ cup granulated sugar
½ cup packed brown sugar
1 large egg
1¾ cups (10-ounce package) NESTLÉ® TOLL HOUSE® Holiday
    Shapes & Morsels, *divided*
    Peanut Butter Frosting and Filling (recipe follows)

PREHEAT oven to 350°F.

COMBINE flour, baking soda and salt in small bowl. Beat butter, peanut butter, granulated sugar, brown sugar and vanilla extract in large mixer bowl until creamy. Beat in egg. Gradually beat in flour mixture. *Stir in 1 cup Shapes & Morsels (set aside remaining Shapes & Morsels).* Drop dough by rounded tablespoon onto ungreased baking sheets. Press down slightly.

BAKE for 10 to 13 minutes or until golden brown. Cool on baking sheets on wire racks for 2 minutes; remove to wire racks to cool completely.

SPREAD Peanut Butter Frosting and Filling on bottom side of one cookie. Place bottom side of a second cookie over frosting creating a cookie sandwich; press down slightly. Frost top of cookie sandwich and *sprinkle with remaining Shapes & Morsels.* Repeat with *remaining* cookies.   *Makes about 20 cookie sandwiches*

Peanut Butter Frosting and Filling: Stir together 1¼ cups prepared vanilla frosting and ¼ cup creamy or chunky peanut butter.

Peanut Butter and Jelly Cookies

1 **Butter Flavor CRISCO® Stick or 1 cup Butter Flavor CRISCO®**
  All-Vegetable Shortening
1 **cup JIF® Creamy Peanut Butter**
1 **teaspoon vanilla**
⅔ **cup firmly packed light brown sugar**
⅓ **cup granulated sugar**
2 **large eggs**
2 **cups all-purpose flour**
1 **cup SMUCKER'S® Strawberry Preserves or any flavor**

1. Heat oven to 350°F.

2. Combine 1 cup shortening, peanut butter and vanilla in food processor fitted with metal blade. Process until well blended and smooth. Add sugars; process until incorporated completely. Add eggs; beat just until blended. Add flour; pulse until dough begins to form ball. *Do not overprocess.*

3. Place dough in medium bowl. Shape ½ tablespoon dough into ball for each cookie. Place 1½ inches apart on ungreased cookie sheets. Press thumb into center of each ball to create deep well. Fill each well with about ½ teaspoon preserves.

4. Bake at 350°F for 10 minutes or until lightly browned and firm. Cool on cookie sheets 4 minutes; transfer to cooling racks. Leave on racks about 30 minutes or until completely cool.

Makes about 5 dozen cookies

Make It Special

What could be better than Peanut Butter and Jelly Cookies and milk. Purchase individual cartons of reduced-fat milk. Provide colorful straws to go with this nutritious drink and colorful napkins for this delicious cookie. Simple, familiar foods often are the best treat.

Peanut Butter Chips and Jelly Bars

1½ **cups all-purpose flour**
½ **cup sugar**
¾ **teaspoon baking powder**
½ **cup (1 stick) cold butter or margarine**
1 **egg, beaten**
¾ **cup grape jelly**
1⅔ **cups (10-ounce package) REESE'S® Peanut Butter Chips, divided**

1. Heat oven to 375°F. Grease 9-inch square baking pan.

2. Stir together flour, sugar and baking powder in large bowl. With pastry blender or two knives, cut in butter until mixture resembles coarse crumbs. Add egg; blend well. Reserve 1 cup mixture; press remaining mixture onto bottom of prepared pan. Stir jelly to soften; spread evenly over crust. Sprinkle 1 cup peanut butter chips over jelly. Stir together reserved crumb mixture with remaining ⅔ cup chips; sprinkle over top.

3. Bake 25 to 30 minutes or until lightly browned. Cool completely in pan on wire rack. Cut into bars.   *Makes about 16 bars*

⚘ Make It Special

Serve the best-shaped cookies in town. Use cookie cutters to cut out shapes from these and other bars cookies for a whimsical twist. Make shapes like stars, circles, letters or the school mascot to suit your party theme.

Novelty Sweets

Journey to the land of make-believe where simple cakes and cookies are transformed into stunning creations. Kids' eyes will light up with excitement when they discover these special-shaped, colorfully decorated treats.

Dino-Mite Dinosaurs

    1 cup (2 sticks) butter, softened
1¼ cups granulated sugar
    1 large egg
    2 squares (1 ounce each) semi-sweet chocolate, melted
    ½ teaspoon vanilla extract
2⅓ cups all-purpose flour
    1 teaspoon baking powder
    ¼ teaspoon salt
    1 cup white frosting
       Assorted food colorings
    1 cup "M&M's"® Chocolate Mini Baking Bits

In large bowl cream butter and sugar until light and fluffy; beat in egg, chocolate and vanilla. In medium bowl combine flour, baking powder and salt; add to creamed mixture. Wrap and refrigerate dough 2 to 3 hours. Preheat oven to 350°F. Working with half the dough at a time on lightly floured surface, roll to ¼-inch thickness. Cut into dinosaur shapes using 4-inch cookie cutters. Place about 2 inches apart on ungreased cookie sheets. Bake 10 to 12 minutes. Cool 2 minutes on cookie sheets; cool completely on wire racks. Tint frosting to desired colors. Frost cookies and decorate with "M&M's"® Chocolate Mini Baking Bits. Store in tightly covered container.   *Makes 24 cookies*

Juke Box Cake

**1 package (about 18 ounces) chocolate fudge cake mix, plus
    ingredients to prepare mix**
**1 container (16 ounces) buttercream frosting, divided
    Red and yellow food coloring**
1 container (12 ounces) whipped milk chocolate frosting
1 tube (4¼ ounces) black decorating icing plus plain decorating tip

1. Preheat oven to 350°F. Grease and flour 13×9-inch cake pan; set aside.

2. Prepare cake mix according to package directions. Pour batter evenly into prepared pan. Bake 35 minutes or until wooden pick inserted into center comes out clean.

3. Cool cake in pan on wire rack 10 minutes. Remove cake to wire rack; cool completely.

4. Meanwhile, color frostings. Place ¼ cup buttercream frosting in small bowl; tint red with red food coloring (about 20 drops). In another small bowl, add ¼ cup buttercream frosting; tint orange using 6 drops red and 8 drops yellow food coloring. Place each in pastry bags fitted with plain tips (#5 or 6) or resealable plastic food storage bags with 1 corner cut off.

5. Using paper plate as a guide, cut top of juke box into rounded shape. (Refer to diagram.)

6. Frost entire cake with chocolate frosting. Use some of remaining buttercream frosting to create semicircular background for records and wedge-shaped background for speakers. Using orange frosting, pipe small section above semicircle and grate on speaker section.

7. Place remaining buttercream frosting into pastry bag fitted with basket weave tip (#48); pipe 2 panels between record area and speaker section.

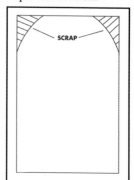

8. Use black decorating icing fitted with plain decorating tip to add additional details.

9. Pipe red and orange stripes around edges of juke box. *Makes 20 servings*

Mice Creams

1 **pint vanilla ice cream**
1 **(4-ounce) package READY CRUST® Mini-Graham Cracker Pie Crusts**
Ears—12 KEEBLER® Grasshopper® cookies
Tails—3 chocolate twigs, broken in half *or* **6 (3-inch) pieces black shoestring licorice**
Eyes and noses—18 brown candy-coated chocolate candies
Whiskers—2 teaspoons chocolate sprinkles

Place 1 scoop vanilla ice cream into each crust. Press cookie ears and tails into ice cream. Press eyes, noses, and whiskers in place. Serve immediately. Do not refreeze. *Makes 6 servings*

Prep Time: 15 minutes

Leapin' Lizards!

1 **cup butterscotch-flavor chips**
½ **cup corn syrup**
3 **tablespoons butter**
1 **cup white chocolate chips**
Green food coloring
7 **cups crisp rice cereal**
Candy corn, green jelly beans, red miniature jaw breakers and chocolate chips

1. Line baking sheet with waxed paper.

2. Combine butterscotch chips, corn syrup and butter in large saucepan. Stir over medium heat until chips are melted. Add white chocolate chips and green food coloring; stir well. Remove from heat. Add cereal; stir to coat evenly.

3. Lightly butter hands and shape about 1½ cups cereal mixture into lizard (about 6 inches long). Place on prepared baking sheet. Decorate with candies. Repeat with remaining mixture. *Makes 4 lizards*

Sunshine Butter Cookies

¾ cup (1½ sticks) butter, softened
¾ cup sugar
1 egg
2¼ cups all-purpose flour
¼ teaspoon salt
Grated peel of ½ lemon
1 teaspoon frozen lemonade concentrate, thawed
Lemonade Royal Icing (recipe page 84)
Thin pretzel sticks
Yellow paste food coloring
Gummy fruit and black licorice strings

1. Beat butter and sugar in large bowl at high speed of electric mixer until fluffy. Add egg; beat well.

2. Combine flour, salt and lemon peel in medium bowl. Add to butter mixture. Stir in lemonade concentrate. Refrigerate 2 hours.

3. Prepare Lemonade Royal Icing. Cover; let stand at room temperature. Preheat oven to 350°F. Grease cookie sheets.

4. Roll dough on floured surface to ⅛-inch thickness. Cut out cookies using 3-inch round cookie cutter. Place cookies on prepared cookie sheets. Press pretzel sticks into edges of cookies to resemble sunshine rays; press gently. Bake 10 minutes or until lightly browned. Remove to wire racks; cool completely.

5. Add food coloring to Lemonade Royal Icing. Spoon about ½ cup icing into resealable plastic food storage bag; seal. Cut tiny tip from corner of bag. Pipe thin circle around flat side of each cookie to create outline.

6. Add water, 1 tablespoon at a time, to remaining icing in bowl until thick but pourable consistency. Spoon icing in cookie centers staying within outline.

7. Decorate cookies with gummy fruit and licorice to make "sunny" faces. Let stand 1 hour or until dry.   *Makes about 36 cookies*

continued on page 84

Sunshine Butter Cookies, continued

Lemonade Royal Icing

3¾ cups sifted powdered sugar
3 tablespoons meringue powder
6 tablespoons frozen lemonade concentrate, thawed

Beat all ingredients in large bowl at high speed of electric mixer until smooth.

Ghosts on a Stick

4 wooden craft sticks
4 medium pears, stems removed
9 squares (2 ounces each) almond bark
Mini chocolate chips

● Line baking sheet with waxed paper and 4 paper baking cups. Insert wooden sticks into stem ends of pears.

● Melt almond bark according to package directions.

● Dip one pear into melted almond bark, spooning bark over top to coat evenly. Remove excess by scraping pear bottom across rim of measuring cup. Place on paper baking cup; let set 1 minute.

● Decorate with mini chocolate chips to make ghost face. Repeat with remaining pears. Place spoonful of extra almond bark at bottom of pears for ghost tails. Refrigerate until firm.   *Makes 4 servings*

ABC Cookies

- ½ cup (1 stick) butter, softened
- ½ cup granulated sugar
- 1 large egg
- 2 tablespoons orange juice
- 1½ cups all-purpose flour
- 1 teaspoon grated orange peel
- ½ teaspoon baking powder
- ⅛ teaspoon salt
- Orange Icing (recipe follows)
- 1 cup "M&M's"® Chocolate Mini Baking Bits

In large bowl cream butter and sugar until light and fluffy; beat in egg and orange juice. In medium bowl combine flour, orange peel, baking powder and salt; add to creamed mixture. Wrap and refrigerate dough 2 to 3 hours. Preheat oven to 350°F. Working with half the dough at a time on well-floured surface, roll to ¼-inch thickness. Cut into letter shapes using 1½-inch cookie cutters. Place about 2 inches apart on ungreased cookie sheets. Bake 8 to 10 minutes. Cool 1 minute on cookie sheets; cool completely on wire racks. Prepare Orange Icing; spread over cookies. Decorate with "M&M's"® Chocolate Mini Baking Bits. Store in tightly covered container.   *Makes about 84 cookies*

Orange Icing: In medium bowl combine 1 cup powdered sugar, 1 tablespoon water and 1 tablespoon pulp-free orange juice. Add additional water, 1 teaspoon at a time, if necessary to make icing spreadable.

Save Time

You can find specialty cookie cutters in the cake decorating section of craft stores. If you are in a hurry, cut the dough into circles or squares. Bake and frost as above. Then use tubes of colorful frosting to print names, letters or numbers on the top.

Handprints

1 package (20 ounces) refrigerated cookie dough, any flavor
All-purpose flour (optional)
Cookie glazes, frostings and assorted candies

1. Grease cookie sheets. Remove dough from wrapper according to package directions.

2. Cut dough into 4 equal sections. Reserve 1 section; refrigerate remaining 3 sections. Sprinkle reserved dough with flour to minimize sticking, if necessary.

3. Roll dough on prepared cookie sheet to 5×7-inch rectangle.

4. Place hand, palm-side down, on dough. Carefully, cut around outline of hand with knife. Remove scraps. Separate fingers as much as possible using small spatula. Pat fingers outward to lengthen slightly. Repeat steps with remaining dough.

5. Freeze dough 15 minutes. Preheat oven to 350°F.

6. Bake 7 to 13 minutes or until cookies are set and edges are golden brown. Cool completely on cookie sheets.

7. Decorate as desired.   *Makes 5 large handprint cookies*

Make It Special

To get the kids involved, let them use their hands to make the handprints. Trace an outline of each kids hands on waxed paper. Label and use to cut out cookie dough. The kids will enjoy seeing how their handprints bake into big cookies. For a less time-intensive project. Use one size hand for all the cookies; then allow the kids to individually decorate their cookie.

Ice Cream Cone Cakes

    1 **package DUNCAN HINES® Moist Deluxe® Cake Mix (any flavor)**
    1 **container DUNCAN HINES® Creamy Home-Style Chocolate**
        Frosting
    1 **container DUNCAN HINES® Creamy Home-Style Vanilla Frosting**
        Chocolate sprinkles
        Assorted decors
        Jelly beans
    2 **maraschino cherries, for garnish**

1. Preheat oven to 350°F. Grease and flour one 8-inch round cake pan and one 8-inch square pan.

2. Prepare cake following package directions for basic recipe. Pour about 2 cups batter into round pan. Pour about 3 cups batter into square pan. Bake at 350°F for 30 to 35 minutes or until toothpick inserted in center comes out clean. Cool following package directions.

3. To assemble, cut cooled cake and arrange as shown. Frost "cone" with Chocolate frosting, reserving ½ cup. Place writing tip in pastry bag. Fill with remaining ½ cup Chocolate frosting. Pipe waffle pattern onto "cones." Decorate with chocolate sprinkles. Spread Vanilla frosting on "ice cream." Decorate with assorted decors and jelly beans. Top each with maraschino cherry. *Makes 12 to 16 servings*

Tip: Use tip of knife to draw lines in frosting for waffle pattern as guide for piping chocolate frosting.

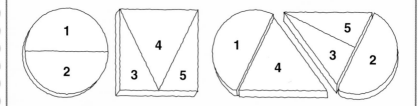

Fruity Cookie Rings and Twists

1 package (20 ounces) refrigerated sugar cookie dough
3 cups fruit-flavored cereal, crushed and divided

1. Remove dough from wrapper according to package directions. Combine dough and ½ cup crushed cereal in large bowl. Divide dough into 32 balls. Refrigerate 1 hour.

2. Preheat oven to 375°F. Shape dough balls into 6- to 8-inch-long ropes. Roll ropes in remaining cereal to coat; shape into rings or fold in half and twist.

3. Place cookies 2 inches apart on ungreased cookie sheets.

4. Bake 10 to 11 minutes or until lightly browned. Remove to wire racks; cool completely.

Makes 32 cookies

Tip: These cookie rings can be transformed into Christmas tree ornaments by poking a hole in each unbaked ring using a drinking straw. Bake cookies and decorate with colored gels and small candies to resemble wreaths. Loop thin ribbon through holes and tie ends together.

Sparkling Magic Wands

1 package (18 ounces) refrigerated sugar cookie dough
48 pretzel sticks (2½ inches long)
Prepared colored decorating icings
Colored sugar or edible glitter and gold dragées

1. Preheat oven to 350°F. Remove dough from wrapper.

2. Roll dough to ⅛-inch thickness on well-floured surface. Cut dough with 2-inch star-shaped cookie cutter. Place each star on top of 1 pretzel stick; press lightly to attach. Place on ungreased cookie sheet.

3. Bake 4 to 6 minutes or until edges are lightly browned. Carefully remove to wire rack; cool completely.

4. Spread icing on stars; sprinkle with colored sugar. Press dragées into points of stars. Let stand until set.

Makes 48 cookies

Igloo Cake

1 package (about 18 ounces) white cake mix plus
    ingredients to prepare mix
1 cup marshmallow creme
1 container (16 ounces) white frosting, divided
1 snack-size plain cake donut
  Blue food coloring
  White cake glitter
  Rock candy
  Plastic polar bear and penguin figurines (optional)

1. Preheat oven to 350°F. Grease and lightly flour 8-inch heatproof ceramic or metal mixing bowl.

2. Prepare cake mix according to package directions. Pour batter evenly into bowl. Bake 50 to 55 minutes or until cake tester or bamboo skewer inserted into center of cake comes out clean.

3. Cool in pan on wire rack 10 minutes. Remove cake to wire rack; cool completely.

4. Using serrated knife, divide cake horizontally into 2 layers. Place bottom layer on serving plate.

5. Using long spatula lightly sprayed with cooking spray, spread marshmallow creme on bottom cake layer to within ½ inch of edge. Stack top cake layer on top.

6. Remove ¼ cup frosting from container; set aside. Use most of remaining frosting to frost cake. Attach donut to base of cake to form entrance to igloo; frost completely.

7. Color reserved frosting with blue food coloring and place in a pastry bag fitted with #7 plain tip. Pipe frosting in circular strips around cake, 2 inches apart. Pipe short, vertical strips between horizontal strips to give illusion of blocks of ice. Pipe doorway onto frosted donut.

8. Dust cake with cake glitter to resemble snow. Break chunks of rock candy and scatter around outside of cake. Decorate with plastic polar bear and penguin figurines, if desired. *Makes 16 to 20 servings*

Purse Cake

1 package (about 18 ounces) yellow cake mix, plus ingredients to prepare mix
½ cup seedless raspberry preserves
1 container (16 ounces) white frosting
Red food coloring
Assorted candies: black string licorice, soft licorice pieces, black jelly beans, pastel egg sprinkles, candy bracelet, candy crayons

1. Preheat oven to 350°F. Grease and flour 13×9-inch cake pan; set aside.

2. Prepare cake mix according to package directions. Pour batter evenly into prepared pan. Bake 35 minutes or until wooden pick inserted into center of cake comes out clean.

3. Cool in pan on wire rack 10 minutes. Remove cake from pan to wire rack; cool completely.

4. Use wooden picks to mark sections to be cut (Diagram A). Use serrated knife to cut cake into 4 sections. Discard ½-inch strip of excess cake.

continued on page 96

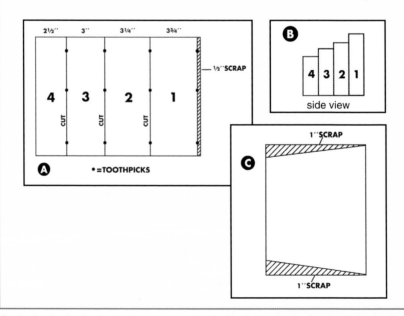

Purse Cake, continued

5. Place widest section (Piece 1), cut side down, on cake board or serving platter. Spread left side of Piece 1 with preserves; attach next-widest section (Piece 2), cut side down, to the left of Piece 1 so layers are stacked sideways. Repeat process for remaining 2 sections. Final cake should gradually slope downward from right to left (Diagram B).

6. Measure 1 inch from side of shortest cake section. Using serrated knife, cut back to corner of tallest section. Repeat on other side of cake. Discard scraps (Diagram C). Cover cake with foil or plastic wrap and freeze several hours before frosting.

7. Tint frosting pink using red food coloring. Remove cake from freezer; frost cake on all sides, filling in graduated slope with frosting.

8. To decorate cake, cut 18-inch piece black string licorice; gently press into frosting to outline purse flap. Cut ½-inch pieces to resemble stitching. Use 5 pink or white licorice candies to create flower petals. Place halved black jelly bean in center of each flower. Place pastel egg sprinkles in groups of 3 to add more texture. To make purse strap, knot 3 long pieces string licorice together. Braid licorice; knot other end. Push knots into frosting on sides of purse. Place candy crayons and bracelets around purse. *Makes 16 to 20 servings*

Make It Special

In addition to traditional birthday candles, decorate cakes with a variety of candies and chocolates such as licorice whips, milk chocolate buttons, rainbow sprinkles, candy-covered chocolates, white chocolate chips, chocolate numbers, glacé cherries and other assorted candies or nonpareils. Use candies to transform plain cakes into realistic pictures.

Shapers

2 packages (20 ounces each) refrigerated sugar cookie dough
Red, yellow, green and blue paste food colorings
1 container (16 ounces) vanilla frosting

1. Remove dough from wrapper according to package directions. Cut each roll of dough in half.

2. Beat ¼ of dough and red food coloring in medium bowl until well blended. Shape red dough into 5-inch log on sheet of waxed paper; set aside.

3. Repeat with remaining dough and food colorings. Cover; refrigerate tinted logs 1 hour or until firm.

4. Roll or shape each log on smooth surface to create circular, triangular, square and oval-shaped logs. Use ruler to keep triangle and square sides flat. Cover; refrigerate dough 1 hour or until firm.

5. Preheat oven to 350°F. Cut shaped dough into ¼-inch slices. Place 2 inches apart on ungreased baking sheets. Bake 9 to 12 minutes. Remove to wire racks; cool completely.

6. Spoon frosting into resealable plastic food storage bag; seal. Cut tiny tip from corner of bag. Pipe frosting around each cookie to define shape.

Makes about 80 cookies

Make It Special

If you have extra liquid food colorings at home, tint the vanilla frosting different colors. Frost cookies using contrasting colored frosting, for example green frosting on a red cookie.

Chocolate X and O Cookies

⅔ **cup butter or margarine, softened**
1 **cup sugar**
2 **teaspoons vanilla extract**
2 **eggs**
2 **tablespoons light corn syrup**
2½ **cups all-purpose flour**
½ **cup HERSHEY'S Cocoa**
½ **teaspoon baking soda**
¼ **teaspoon salt**
  Decorating icing

1. Beat butter, sugar and vanilla in large bowl on medium speed of electric mixer until fluffy. Add eggs; beat well. Beat in corn syrup.

2. Combine flour, cocoa, baking soda and salt; gradually add to butter mixture, beating until well blended. Cover; refrigerate until dough is firm enough to handle.

3. Heat oven to 350°F. Shape dough into X and O shapes. Place on ungreased cookie sheet.

4. Bake 5 minutes or until set. Remove from cookie sheet to wire rack. Cool completely. Decorate as desired with icing.

Makes about 60 cookies

Preparation Hint

To shape X's: Shape rounded teaspoons of dough into 3-inch logs. Place 1 log on cookie sheet; press lightly in center. Place another 3-inch log on top of first one, forming X shape. To shape O's: Shape rounded teaspoon dough into 5-inch logs. Connect ends, pressing lightly, forming O shape.

Drum Layer Cake

    1 **package DUNCAN HINES® Moist Deluxe® Cake Mix (any flavor)**
    1 **container DUNCAN HINES® Creamy Home-Style Classic Vanilla**
        Frosting, divided
        Green food coloring
        Thin pretzel sticks
        Candy-coated chocolate pieces
        Lollipops

1. Preheat oven to 350°F. Grease and flour two 8-inch round cake pans.

2. Prepare, bake and cool cake following package directions for basic recipe.

3. To assemble, place half the Vanilla frosting in small bowl. Tint with green food coloring; set aside. Place one cake layer on serving plate. Spread with half of untinted vanilla frosting. Top with second cake layer. Spread green frosting on sides of cake. Spread remaining Vanilla frosting on top of cake. Arrange pretzel sticks and candy-coated chocolates on sides of cake as shown in photograph. Place lollipops on top of cake for "drumsticks."
Makes 12 to 16 servings

Preparation Hint

For a brighter green frosting, as shown in the photograph, use paste food colors available from cake decorating and specialty shops.

Stripes

5½ **cups cake batter, divided**
1 **(10-inch) round cake board, covered, or large platter**
1 **container (16 ounces) white frosting**
3 **chocolate sandwich cookies**
1 **individual chocolate-covered cake roll**
  Pretzel sticks
  Chocolate sprinkles
  Assorted candies and red licorice whip

1. Preheat oven to 350°F. Grease and flour 9-inch round cake pan and medium muffin pan.

2. Pour 3½ cups cake batter into cake pan; pour remaining cake batter into muffin pan (¼ cup batter per muffin cup). Bake cake in pan 35 to 45 minutes and cupcakes about 20 minutes or until toothpick inserted into centers comes out clean. Cool 15 minutes in pans. Loosen edges; invert onto wire racks and cool completely.

3. Trim tops and sides of round cake and two cupcakes. (Reserve remaining cupcakes for another use.) Place cake on prepared cake board. Position two cupcakes next to cake to form ears.

4. Tint frosting orange. Frost entire cake and cupcakes with orange frosting.

5. Carefully open two sandwich cookies to expose white filling. Place opened cookies on tiger's ears. Cut two thin slices from cake roll; place on tiger's face for eyes.

6. Add pretzel whiskers, cookie nose, candy mouth and chocolate sprinkle stripes as shown in photo. *Makes 12 to 14 servings*

Snowy Owl Cupcakes

1 package (18 ounces) white cake mix, plus ingredients
    to prepare mix
1 container (16 ounces) vanilla frosting
2½ cups sweetened, shredded coconut
48 round gummy candies
24 chocolate-covered coffee beans or black jelly beans
1 tub (0.6 ounce) black piping gel

1. Line standard (2½-inch) muffin cups with paper liners, or spray with nonstick cooking spray.

2. Prepare cake and bake in muffin cups according to directions. Cool in pans on wire racks 15 minutes. Remove cupcakes and cool completely.

3. Frost cupcakes with vanilla frosting. Sprinkle coconut over each cupcake, covering completely. Place 2 gummy candies on each cupcake for eyes. Add chocolate-covered coffee bean for beak. Use piping gel to dot eyes.

Makes 24 cupcakes

Make It Special

Select novelty candles in shapes of numerals, cartoon figures, and also novelty candle holders to quickly decorate a cake.

Holiday Celebrations

Celebrate holidays throughout the year with whimsical, festive treats that fascinate and delight. Draw rave reviews with these fabulous ideas—perfect for any school holiday party.

Cookie Decorating Party

- 1 container (16 ounces) strawberry frosting, at room temperature
- 48 vanilla wafers or sugar cookies
- ¼ to ½ pound assorted Valentine candies, such as cinnamon hearts, conversation hearts, chocolate candies, red hots and heart-shaped sprinkles

Stir frosting in can until soft and creamy. Divide frosting evenly among small paper cups to equal one paper cup per child. Give each child an equal number of cookies, one paper cup of frosting and assortment of candies. Have children dip cookies into frosting or spread frosting with backs of spoons. Decorate with candies or sprinkles as desired.

Makes 48 cookies

 Make It Special

> *Create your own decorating party for any holiday or birthday. Use different colored frostings, holiday candies and fun sprinkles to create themed cookies for every occasion.*

Valentine Stained Glass Hearts

½ cup (1 stick) butter or margarine, softened
¾ cup granulated sugar
2 eggs
1 teaspoon vanilla extract
2⅓ cups all-purpose flour
1 teaspoon baking powder
Red hard candies, crushed (about ⅓ cup)
Frosting (optional)

Cream butter and sugar in mixing bowl. Beat in eggs and vanilla. Sift flour and baking powder together. Gradually stir in flour mixture until dough is very stiff. Cover and chill. Dough needs to chill 3 hours to overnight.

Preheat oven to 375°F. Roll out dough to ⅛-inch thickness on lightly floured surface. To prevent cookies from becoming tough and brittle, do not incorporate too much flour. Cut out cookies using large heart-shaped cookie cutter or use sharp knife and cut heart design. Transfer cookies to foil-lined baking sheet. Using small heart-shaped cookie cutter, cut out and remove heart design from center of each cookie. Fill cutout sections with crushed candy. Bake 7 to 9 minutes or until cookies are lightly browned and candy has melted. Do not overcook.

Remove from oven; immediately slide foil off baking sheet. Cool completely; carefully loosen cookies from foil. If desired, pipe decorative borders with frosting around edges.

Makes about 30 cookies

Favorite recipe from **The Sugar Association, Inc.**

Irish Flag Cookies

1½ cups all-purpose flour
1 teaspoon baking powder
½ teaspoon salt
¾ cup granulated sugar
¾ cup light brown sugar
½ cup (1 stick) butter, softened
2 eggs
2 teaspoons vanilla
1 package (12 ounces) semisweet chocolate chips
Prepared white frosting
Green and orange food coloring

1. Preheat oven to 350°F. Grease 13×9-inch baking pan. Combine flour, baking powder and salt in small bowl; set aside.

2. Beat granulated sugar, brown sugar and butter in large bowl with electric mixer at medium speed until light and fluffy. Beat in eggs and vanilla. Add flour mixture. Beat at low speed until well blended. Stir in chocolate chips. Spread batter evenly into prepared pan. Bake 25 to 30 minutes or until golden brown. Remove pan to wire rack; cool completely. Cut into 3¼×1½-inch bars.

3. Divide frosting among 3 small bowls. Tint 1 with green food coloring and 1 with orange. Leave remaining frosting white. Frost individual cookies to resemble the Irish flag as shown in diagram.

Makes 24 cookies

green	white	orange

St. Pat's Pudding Pies

1 package (4-serving size) pistachio pudding and pie filling
    mix plus ingredients to prepare mix
1 package mini graham cracker pie crusts (6 crusts)
    Assorted candies, colored sprinkles and gumdrops

Prepare pudding according to package directions; divide evenly among crusts. Decorate with candies and sprinkles as desired. Roll gumdrops on heavily sugared surface until fairly flat; cut into shamrock shapes. Place in centers of pies. Refrigerate leftovers. *Makes 6 pies*

Chocolate Bunny Cookies

1 (21-ounce) package DUNCAN HINES® Family-Style
    Chewy Fudge Brownie Mix
1 egg
¼ cup water
¼ cup vegetable oil
1⅓ cups pecan halves (96)
1 container DUNCAN HINES® Creamy Home-Style
    Dark Chocolate Fudge Frosting
    White chocolate chips

1. Preheat oven to 350°F. Grease baking sheets.

2. Combine brownie mix, egg, water and oil in large bowl. Stir with spoon until well blended, about 50 strokes. Drop by level tablespoonfuls 2 inches apart on greased baking sheets. Place two pecan halves, flat-side up, on each cookie for ears. Bake at 350°F for 10 to 12 minutes or until set. Cool 2 minutes on baking sheets. Remove to cooling racks. Cool completely.

3. Spread Dark Chocolate Fudge frosting on one cookie. Place white chocolate chips, upside down, on frosting for eyes and nose. Dot each eye with frosting using toothpick. Repeat for remaining cookies. Allow frosting to set before storing cookies between layers of waxed paper in airtight container. *Makes 48 cookies*

Tip: For variety, frost cookies with Duncan Hines® Vanilla Frosting and use semisweet chocolate chips for the eyes and noses.

Eggs-Cellent Easter Cookies

- 1 package (18 ounces) refrigerated sugar cookie dough
- 1 cup plus 1 tablespoon powdered sugar, divided
- ¼ cup all-purpose flour
- 1 teaspoon almond extract
  Blue food coloring
  Blue sugar (optional)
- 1 package (3 ounces) cream cheese, softened
- 1 tablespoon unsalted butter, softened
  Red food coloring
- ½ cup shredded sweetened coconut (optional)
  Prepared colored decorating icings and decorating gels
  (optional)

1. Preheat oven to 350°F. Grease cookie sheets. Remove dough from wrapper; place in large bowl. Let dough stand at room temperature about 15 minutes.

2. Add 1 tablespoon powdered sugar, flour, almond extract and blue food coloring to dough in bowl; beat at medium speed of electric mixer until well blended and evenly colored.

3. Shape dough into 40 (2½-inch-long) egg shapes; roll in blue sugar, if desired. Place 2 inches apart on prepared cookie sheets.

4. Bake 8 to 10 minutes or until set and edges are lightly browned. Cool on cookie sheets 2 minutes. Remove to wire racks; cool completely.

5. Combine cream cheese, butter, remaining 1 cup powdered sugar and red food coloring (tint pink) in medium bowl; beat at medium speed of electric mixer until smooth. Stir in coconut, if desired.

6. Spread pink filling on 20 cookies. Top with remaining 20 cookies to make sandwiches. Decorate tops of sandwiches as desired with colored icings and gels. Let stand until set. Store in refrigerator.

Makes 20 sandwich cookies

Easter Baskets and Bunnies Cupcakes

  2 cups sugar
1¾ cups all-purpose flour
  ¾ cup HERSHEY'S Cocoa or HERSHEY'S Dutch Processed Cocoa
1½ teaspoons baking powder
1½ teaspoons baking soda
  1 teaspoon salt
  2 eggs
  1 cup milk
  ½ cup vegetable oil
  2 teaspoons vanilla extract
  1 cup boiling water
    Creamy Vanilla Frosting (recipe follows)
    Green, red and yellow food color
3¾ cups MOUNDS® Sweetened Coconut Flakes, divided and tinted*
    Suggested garnishes (marshmallows, HERSHEY'S MINI KISSES™
    Milk Chocolates, licorice, jelly beans)

To tint coconut, combine ¾ teaspoon water with several drops green food color in small bowl. Stir in 1¼ cups coconut. Toss with fork until evenly tinted. Repeat with red and yellow food color and remaining coconut.

1. Heat oven to 350°F. Line muffin cups (2½ inches in diameter) with paper bake cups.

2. Stir together sugar, flour, cocoa, baking powder, baking soda and salt in large bowl. Add eggs, milk, oil and vanilla; beat on medium speed of mixer 2 minutes. Stir in boiling water (batter will be thin). Fill muffin cups ⅔ full with batter.

3. Bake 22 to 25 minutes or until wooden pick inserted in centers comes out clean. Cool completely. Prepare Creamy Vanilla Frosting; frost cupcakes. Immediately press desired color tinted coconut onto each cupcake. Garnish as desired to resemble Easter basket or bunny.

Makes about 33 cupcakes

Creamy Vanilla Frosting: Beat ⅓ cup softened butter or margarine in medium bowl. Add 1 cup powdered sugar and 1½ teaspoons vanilla extract; beat well. Add 2½ cups powdered sugar alternately with ¼ cup milk, beating to spreading consistency. Makes about 2 cups frosting.

Patriotic Cocoa Cupcakes

2 cups sugar
1¾ cups all-purpose flour
¾ cup HERSHEY'S Cocoa
2 teaspoons baking soda
1 teaspoon baking powder
1 teaspoon salt
2 eggs
1 cup buttermilk or sour milk*
1 cup boiling water
½ cup vegetable oil
1 teaspoon vanilla extract
Vanilla Frosting (recipe follows)
Chocolate stars or blue and red decorating icings (in tube)

*To sour milk: Use 1 tablespoon white vinegar plus milk to equal 1 cup.

1. Heat oven to 350°F. Grease and flour muffin cups (2½ inches in diameter) or line with paper bake cups.

2. Combine dry ingredients in large bowl. Add eggs, buttermilk, water, oil and vanilla; beat on medium speed of mixer 2 minutes (batter will be thin). Fill cups ⅔ full with batter.

3. Bake 15 minutes or until wooden pick inserted in centers comes out clean. Remove cupcakes from pan. Cool completely. To make chocolate stars for garnish, if desired, cut several cupcakes into ½-inch slices; cut out star shapes from cake slices. Frost remaining cupcakes. Garnish with chocolate stars or with blue and red decorating icings.

Makes about 30 cupcakes

Vanilla Frosting: Beat ¼ cup (½ stick) softened butter, ¼ cup shortening and 2 teaspoons vanilla extract. Add 1 cup powdered sugar; beat until creamy. Add 3 cups powdered sugar alternately with 3 to 4 tablespoons milk, beating to spreading consistency. Makes about 2⅓ cups frosting.

Firecracker Cake

- 3 packages (18¼ ounces each) cake mix with pudding in the mix (any flavor), plus ingredients to prepare mixes
- 2 cups strawberry spreadable fruit
- 3 containers (16 ounces each) vanilla frosting
  Red and blue paste food colorings
  Licorice whip
- 1 tube (4¼ ounces) white decorator icing with tips

Supplies
- 3 empty 6-ounce aluminum cans, washed, dried and both ends removed

1. Prepare cake mixes according to package directions. Reserve 1 cup batter. Divide remaining batter among 2 (9-inch) greased square baking pans and 4 (7½-inch) greased square disposable baking pans. Generously grease and flour cans. Cover one end of each can tightly with aluminum foil. Pour about ⅓ cup reserved cake batter into each can. Place filled cans on baking sheet.

2. Bake cakes according to package directions. Cool in pans and cans 10 minutes. Remove from pans and cans to wire racks; cool completely. Wrap tightly in plastic wrap; freeze overnight.

3. Trim 2 (7½-inch) cakes to 5-inch squares. Spread one 5-inch cake, one 7½-inch cake and one 9-inch cake with ⅓ cup spreadable fruit each; top each with remaining same-sized cake.

4. Place 1½ containers frosting in medium bowl; tint with red food coloring. Place ½ container frosting in small bowl; tint with blue food coloring. Frost sides of 9-inch cake with red frosting; frost top with white frosting. Frost 1 side of 7½-inch cake with blue frosting; frost remaining sides with white frosting. DO NOT FROST TOP. Frost 1 side of 5-inch cake with blue frosting; frost remaining sides with red frosting and frost top with white frosting. Frost can cakes one each with red, white and blue frosting.

5. Place 9-inch cake on serving platter. Top with 7½-inch cake, turning at an angle to the right. Frost top right corner of 7½-inch cake with blue frosting as shown in photo. Frost the rest of the top of the middle layer white. Add 5-inch cake as top layer, also twisting to the right at the same angle.

continued on page 120

Firecracker Cake, continued

6. Add firecrackers to cake top, cutting ends at angles as necessary. Place remaining frosting in small resealable plastic food storage bags. Cut off tiny corner of each bag; pipe onto firecrackers as desired. Place small piece of licorice in each firecracker for fuse. Pipe border around base and top of cake, and up sides with white decorator icing.

Makes 30 servings

Cherry Oatmeal Bars

- ¾ cup (1½ sticks) butter or margarine
- 2 cups firmly packed brown sugar
- 2 cups all-purpose flour
- 2 cups old-fashioned or quick-cooking oats, uncooked
- 2 teaspoons baking soda
- 1 (21-ounce) can cherry pie filling
- 2 tablespoons granulated sugar
- 1 tablespoon cornstarch
- ½ teaspoon almond extract

Put butter and brown sugar in a large mixing bowl. Beat with an electric mixer on medium speed 3 to 4 minutes, or until well mixed. Combine flour, oats and baking soda. Add flour mixture to sugar mixture; mix on low speed until crumbly.

Spread two-thirds of the oats mixture into the bottom of an ungreased 13×9×2-inch baking pan. Press down to make a firm layer.

Purée cherry pie filling with an electric blender or food processor until smooth. Pour puréed filling into a medium saucepan. Combine granulated sugar and cornstarch; stir into filling. Cook, stirring constantly, over low heat until mixture is thick and bubbly. Stir in almond extract. Pour cherry mixture evenly over oats layer. Crumble remaining oats mixture evenly over cherry layer.

Bake in a preheated 350°F oven 30 to 35 minutes, or until golden brown. Let cool before cutting into bars. *Makes 32 to 40 bars*

Favorite recipe from **Cherry Marketing Institute**

Jumbo Jack-o'-Lantern Brownie

¾ cup (1½ sticks) butter or margarine, melted
1½ cups sugar
1½ teaspoons vanilla extract
3 eggs
¾ cup all-purpose flour
½ cup HERSHEY'S Cocoa
½ teaspoon baking powder
¼ teaspoon salt
Orange Buttercream Frosting (recipe follows)
Decorating icing or gel and assorted candies

1. Heat oven to 350°F. Line 12-inch pizza pan with foil; grease foil.

2. Stir together butter, sugar and vanilla in medium bowl. Add eggs; with spoon, beat well. Stir together flour, cocoa, baking powder and salt; gradually add to egg mixture, stirring until well blended. Spread batter into prepared pan.

3. Bake 20 to 22 minutes or until top springs back when touched lightly in center. Cool completely in pan on wire rack.

4. Remove brownie from pan; peel off foil. Prepare Orange Buttercream Frosting; spread over top of brownie. Garnish as desired with decorating icing and candies to resemble jack-o'-lantern face.

Makes 12 to 15 servings

Orange Buttercream Frosting

3 tablespoons butter or margarine, softened
2 cups powdered sugar
2 tablespoons milk
½ teaspoon vanilla extract
Red and yellow food colors

Beat butter in small bowl until creamy. Gradually add powdered sugar, milk and vanilla, beating until smooth and of spreading consistency. Add additional milk, 1 teaspoon at a time, if needed. Stir in food colors for desired orange color. Makes 1 cup frosting.

Spider Cupcakes

- 1 package (18¼ ounces) yellow or white cake mix
- 1 cup solid-pack pumpkin
- ¾ cup water
- 3 eggs
- 2 tablespoons oil
- 1 teaspoon ground cinnamon
- 1 teaspoon pumpkin pie spice*
  Orange food coloring
- 1 container (16 ounces) vanilla, cream cheese or caramel frosting
- ⅔ cup (4 ounces) semisweet chocolate
- 48 black gumdrops

Substitute ½ teaspoon ground cinnamon, ¼ teaspoon ground ginger and ⅛ teaspoon each ground allspice and ground nutmeg for 1 teaspoon pumpkin pie spice.

1. Preheat oven to 350°F. Line 24 standard (2½-inch) muffin pan cups with paper baking liners, or spray with nonstick cooking spray.

2. Combine cake mix, pumpkin, water, eggs, oil, cinnamon and pumpkin pie spice in bowl. Beat at medium speed of electric mixer 3 minutes or until blended. Spoon ¼ cup batter into each cup. Bake 20 minutes or until toothpicks inserted into centers come out clean. Cool 10 minutes on wire rack. Remove from pan; cool completely.

3. Add orange food coloring to frosting. Stir until well blended; adjust color as needed by adding additional food coloring 1 drop at a time, blending well after each addition. Frost cupcakes.

4. Place chocolate in small resealable plastic food storage bag. Microwave at MEDIUM (50% power) 40 seconds. Knead bag; microwave 30 seconds to 1 minute or until chocolate is melted. Knead bag until chocolate is smooth. Cut tiny corner off one end of bag. Drizzle chocolate in four or five concentric circles over top of cupcake. Immediately draw 6 to 8 lines from center to edges of cupcake with toothpick or knife at regular intervals to make web. Repeat with remaining cupcakes and chocolate.

5. For spider, place one gumdrop in center of web design on top of cupcake. Roll out another gumdrop with rolling pin. Slice thinly and roll into "legs." Place legs onto cupcake to complete spider. Repeat with remaining gumdrops and cupcakes. *Makes 24 cupcakes*

Little Devils

   1 **package (18¼ ounces) carrot cake mix**
   ½ **cup solid-pack pumpkin**
   ⅓ **cup vegetable oil**
   3 **eggs**
   1 **container (16 ounces) cream cheese frosting**
    Assorted Halloween candies, jelly beans and chocolate candies

1. Preheat oven to 350°F. Line 18 standard (2½-inch) or 36 miniature (1¾-inch) muffin cups with paper baking cups.

2. Prepare cake mix according to package directions, using water as directed on package, pumpkin, oil and eggs. Spoon batter into prepared muffin cups. Bake 20 minutes or until toothpick inserted in centers of cupcakes comes out clean. Cool in pans on wire racks 5 minutes; remove and cool completely.

3. Frost cupcakes with frosting. Let each student decorate their own cupcake with assorted candies. *Makes 18 cupcakes*

 Save Time

Most cupcakes and bars freeze well for several months. Store unfrosted in sealed plastic food storage bags or airtight containers. Thaw unwrapped at room temperature before frosting and decorating.

Magical Wizard Hats

1 **package (18¼ ounces) cake mix (any flavor), plus ingredients to prepare mix**
2 **containers (16 ounces each) vanilla frosting**
   Yellow and purple or black food colorings
2 **packages (4 ounces each) sugar cones**
   Orange sugar, silver dragées and black decorating gel

1. Line 24 standard (2½-inch) muffin cups with paper baking cups. Prepare and bake cake mix in muffin cups according to package directions. Cool in pans on wire racks 15 minutes. Remove cupcakes from pan; cool completely.

2. Frost cupcakes with vanilla frosting. Place ½ cup remaining frosting in small bowl; tint with yellow food coloring. Tint remaining frosting with purple or black food coloring. Lightly spread sugar cones with dark frosting; cover completely. Place 1 cone upside down on each frosted cupcake. Spoon yellow frosting into small resealable plastic food storage bag. Cut off 1 small corner of bag. Pipe yellow frosting around base of each frosted cone. Decorate as desired.

Makes 24 cupcakes

Hanukkah Cookies

½ cup (1 stick) unsalted butter, softened
1 package (3 ounces) cream cheese
½ cup sugar
¼ cup honey
1 egg
½ teaspoon vanilla
2½ cups all-purpose flour
⅓ cup finely ground walnuts
1 teaspoon baking powder
¼ teaspoon salt
Blue, yellow and white icings

1. Beat butter, cream cheese, sugar, honey, egg and vanilla in large bowl at medium speed of electric mixer until creamy. Stir in flour, walnuts, baking powder and salt until well blended. Form dough into ball; wrap in plastic wrap and flatten. Refrigerate about 2 hours or until firm.

2. Preheat oven to 350°F. Lightly grease cookie sheets. Roll out dough, small portion at a time, to ¼-inch thickness on floured surface with lightly floured rolling pin. (Keep remaining dough wrapped in refrigerator.) Cut dough with 2½-inch dreidel-shaped cookie cutter and 6-pointed star cookie cutter. Place 2 inches apart on prepared cookie sheets.

3. Bake 8 to 10 minutes or until edges are lightly browned. Let cookies stand on cookie sheets 1 to 2 minutes; transfer to wire racks to cool completely. Decorate cookies with icings.   *Makes about 40 cookies*

Holiday Cookies on a Stick

2¼ cups all-purpose flour
1 teaspoon baking soda
1 teaspoon salt
1 cup (2 sticks) butter, softened
¾ cup granulated sugar
¾ cup packed brown sugar
1 teaspoon vanilla extract
2 large eggs
1¾ cups (10-ounce package) NESTLÉ® TOLL HOUSE® Holiday
    Shapes & Morsels, *divided*
12 wooden craft sticks
1 can (16 ounces) cream cheese frosting

PREHEAT oven to 350°F.

COMBINE flour, baking soda and salt in small bowl. Beat butter, granulated sugar, brown sugar and vanilla extract in large mixer bowl until creamy. Add eggs, one at a time, beating well after each addition. Gradually beat in flour mixture. *Stir in ¾ cup Shapes & Morsels (set aside remaining Shapes & Morsels).* Drop dough by level ⅓ cup measure 3 inches apart on ungreased baking sheets. Shape into mounds with floured fingers; press down slightly. Insert wooden stick into side of each mound.

BAKE for 14 to 18 minutes or until golden brown. Cool on baking sheets on wire racks for 3 minutes; remove to wire racks to cool completely.

SPREAD frosting on tops of cookies. *Sprinkle with remaining Shapes & Morsels.*   *Makes about 12 large cookies*

Gingerbread House

5¼ cups all-purpose flour
 1 tablespoon ground ginger
 2 teaspoons baking soda
1½ teaspoons allspice
 1 teaspoon salt
 2 cups packed dark brown sugar
 1 cup plus 2 tablespoons butter or margarine, softened, divided
 ¾ cup dark corn syrup
 2 large eggs
   Meringue Powder Royal Icing (recipe page 134)
   Assorted candies, peppermint sticks and licorice

1. Draw patterns for house on cardboard, using diagrams on page 134 as guides; cut out patterns. Preheat oven to 375°F. Grease large cookie sheet.

2. Combine flour, ginger, baking soda, allspice and salt in medium bowl. Beat brown sugar and 1 cup butter in large bowl with electric mixer at medium speed until light and fluffy. Beat in corn syrup and eggs. Gradually add flour mixture. Beat at low speed until well blended.

3. Roll about ¼ of dough directly onto prepared cookie sheet to ¼-inch thickness. Lay sheet of waxed paper over dough. Place patterns over waxed paper 2 inches apart. Cut dough around patterns with sharp knife; remove waxed paper. Reserve scraps to reroll with next batch of dough.

4. Bake 15 minutes or until no indentation remains when cookie is touched in center. While cookies are still hot, place cardboard pattern lightly over cookie; trim edges to straighten. Let stand on cookie sheet 5 minutes. Remove cookies to wire racks; cool completely. Repeat with remaining pattern pieces.

5. Cover 12-inch square piece of heavy cardboard with aluminum foil to use as base for house.

6. Prepare Meringue Powder Royal Icing. If desired, some icing may be divided into small bowls and tinted with food coloring to use for decorative piping. Place icing in small resealable plastic freezer bag. Cut off small corner of bag. Pipe icing on edges of all pieces including bottom; "glue" house together at seams and onto base.

continued on page 134

Gingerbread House ✲ 133

Gingerbread House, continued

7. Pipe door and windows onto house. Decorate as desired with icing and candies. If desired, dust house with sifted powdered sugar to resemble snow. *Makes 1 gingerbread house*

Meringue Powder Royal Icing

¼ cup meringue powder*
6 tablespoons water
1 box (16 ounces) powdered sugar, sifted

*Meringue powder is available where cake decorating supplies are sold.

1. Beat meringue powder and water in medium bowl with electric mixer at low speed until well blended. Beat at high speed until stiff peaks form.

2. Beat in sugar at low speed until well blended. Beat at high speed until icing is very stiff. Cover icing with damp cloth to prevent icing from drying. *Makes about 2½ cups*

Note: Meringue Powder Royal Icing is used to glue the house together. It hardens after 5 minutes and completely dries in 20 to 30 minutes.

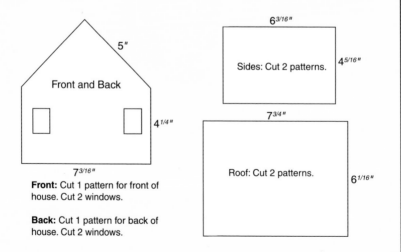

Front and Back

5"

4 1/4"

7 3/16"

Front: Cut 1 pattern for front of house. Cut 2 windows.

Back: Cut 1 pattern for back of house. Cut 2 windows.

6 3/16"

Sides: Cut 2 patterns.

4 5/16"

7 3/4"

Roof: Cut 2 patterns.

6 1/16"

Kringle's Cutouts

⅔ **Butter Flavor CRISCO® Stick or ⅔ cup Butter Flavor CRISCO® All-Vegetable Shortening**
¾ **cup sugar**
1 **tablespoon plus 1 teaspoon milk**
1 **teaspoon vanilla**
1 **egg**
2 **cups all-purpose flour**
1½ **teaspoons baking powder**
¼ **teaspoon salt**

1. Cream shortening, sugar, milk and vanilla in large bowl at medium speed of electric mixer until well blended. Beat in egg. Combine flour, baking powder and salt. Mix into creamed mixture. Cover; refrigerate several hours or overnight.

2. Heat oven to 375°F. Place sheets of foil on countertop for cooling cookies.

3. Roll dough, half at a time, to ⅛-inch thickness on floured surface. Cut into desired shapes. Place cookies 2 inches apart on ungreased cookie sheet. Sprinkle with colored sugar and decors, or leave plain to frost when cool.

4. Bake at 375°F for 7 to 9 minutes. *Do not overbake.* Cool 2 minutes on baking sheet. Remove cookies to foil to cool completely.

Makes about 36 cookies

 Preparation Hint

Cut out cookies make any party special. Use a floured pastry cloth and rolling pin cover to make rolling out the dough easier and to avoid incorporating too much flour into the dough.

Christmas Wreaths

1 **package (18 ounces) refrigerated sugar cookie dough**
2 **tablespoons all-purpose flour**
  Green food coloring
  Red decorating icing
  Green colored sugar or sprinkles

1. Remove dough from wrapper; place in large bowl. Let dough stand at room temperature about 15 minutes.

2. Add flour and green food coloring to dough in bowl; beat at medium speed of electric mixer until dough well blended and evenly colored. Divide dough in half; wrap both halves in plastic wrap and freeze 20 minutes.

3. Preheat oven to 350°F. Grease cookie sheets. For cookie bottoms, roll 1 dough half on lightly floured surface to ⅜-inch thickness. Cut with 3-inch round or fluted cookie cutter; place 2 inches apart on prepared cookie sheets. Using 1-inch round cookie cutter, cut center circle from each cookie.

4. For cookie tops, roll remaining dough half on lightly floured surface to ⅜-inch thickness. Cut with 3-inch round or fluted cookie cutter; place 2 inches apart on prepared cookie sheets. Using 1-inch round cookie cutter, cut center circle from each cookie. Using hors d'oeuvre cutters, miniature cookie cutters or knife, cut tiny circles in half of cutouts. Decorate with green sugar or sprinkles as desired.

5. Bake cutouts 10 minutes or until very lightly browned at edges. Cool on cookie sheet 5 minutes; transfer to wire racks to cool completely.

6. To assemble, spread icing onto flat sides of bottom cookies; place top cookies over icing.   *Makes about 18 sandwich cookies*

Let it Snow

- 2 (9-inch) round cake layers
- 2 (10-inch) round cake boards, taped together and covered, or large tray
- 1½ cups prepared white frosting
- ½ cup prepared chocolate frosting
- Assorted gumdrops
- 1 sugar ice cream cone, cut in half crosswise
- Red pull-apart licorice twists

1. Cut off small piece from one side of each cake layer to form flat edge (so cake layers will fit together as shown in photo).

2. Using diagram as guide, draw pattern for snowman's head (with hat) on 9-inch circle of waxed paper. Cut out pattern and place on top half of cake. Cut out head. Place head and body of snowman on prepared cake board; attach flat edges of cake layers with small amount of white frosting.

3. Frost hat with chocolate frosting. Frost remaining cake with white frosting.

4. Decorate snowman with assorted gumdrops and ice cream cone nose as shown in photo. Arrange licorice to resemble hatband and scarf as shown in photo.   *Makes 16 to 18 servings*

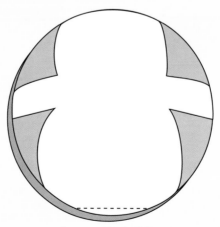

Snowman Head with Hat

Yuletide Layer Bars

½ cup (1 stick) butter
2½ cups graham cracker crumbs
1½ cups chopped nuts
1½ cups flaked coconut
1¾ cups (10-ounce package) NESTLÉ® TOLL HOUSE® Holiday
 Shapes & Morsels
1 can (14 ounces) NESTLÉ® CARNATION® Sweetened
 Condensed Milk

PREHEAT oven to 350°F.

MELT butter in 13×9-inch baking pan in oven; remove from oven. Sprinkle graham cracker crumbs over butter. Stir well; press onto bottom of pan. Sprinkle with nuts, coconut and Shapes & Morsels. Pour sweetened condensed milk evenly over top.

BAKE for 25 to 30 minutes or until light golden brown. Cool completely in pan on wire rack.

Makes 24 to 36 bars

Save Time

Bar cookies are some of the easiest cookies to make since they bake all at once rather than in batches on cookie sheets. Most bar cookies should cool in the pan on a wire rack until barely warm before cutting. Try cutting bar cookies into triangles or diamonds for festive new shapes.

Chocolate Reindeer

    1 cup (2 sticks) butter, softened
    1 cup granulated sugar
    1 egg
    1 teaspoon vanilla
    2 ounces semisweet chocolate, melted
2¼ cups all-purpose flour
    1 teaspoon baking powder
  ¼ teaspoon salt
    Meringue Powder Royal Icing (recipe page 134)
      or prepared white icing
    Assorted food colorings
    Assorted small candies

1. Beat butter and sugar in large bowl at high speed of electric mixer until fluffy. Beat in egg and vanilla. Add melted chocolate; mix well. Add flour, baking powder and salt; mix well. Divide dough in half; wrap each half in plastic wrap and refrigerate 2 hours or until firm.

2. Preheat oven to 325°F. Grease 2 cookie sheets; set aside.

3. Roll one half of dough on well-floured surface to ¼-inch thickness. Cut out cookies with reindeer cookie cutter. Place 2 inches apart on prepared cookie sheets. Chill 10 minutes.

4. Bake 13 to 15 minutes or until set. Cool completely on cookie sheets. Repeat steps with remaining dough.

5. Prepare Meringue Powder Royal Icing. Tint with food colorings as desired. Pipe icing on reindeer and decorate with small candies. For best results, let cookies dry overnight uncovered before storing in airtight container at room temperature.   *Makes 16 (4-inch) cookies*

Note: Use this dough to make cookies to celebrate other holidays. Substitute different holiday-shaped cookie cutters for the reindeer cutters.

Hold the Peanuts!

Solve the dilemma of preparing snacks that meet special dietary needs with this collection of recipes for reduced-fat, reduced-sugar, nut-free or dairy-free treats. The entire class will love these irresistible snacks.

Gingerbread Squares [nut-free/reduced-fat]

- 3 tablespoons margarine, softened
- 2 tablespoons light brown sugar
- ¼ cup molasses
- 1 egg white
- 1¼ cups all-purpose flour
- ½ teaspoon baking soda
- ½ teaspoon ground ginger
- ½ teaspoon ground cinnamon
- ¼ teaspoon salt
- 1 cup sweetened applesauce
- Decorations: tube frostings, colored sugars, red hot cinnamon candies or other small candies (optional)

1. Preheat oven to 350°F. Spray 8-inch square baking pan with nonstick cooking spray; set aside.

2. Beat margarine and sugar in medium bowl until well blended. Beat in molasses and egg white.

3. Combine dry ingredients in small bowl; mix well. Add to margarine mixture alternately with applesauce, mixing well after each addition. Transfer batter to prepared pan.

4. Bake 25 to 30 minutes or until toothpick inserted into center comes out clean. Cool completely on wire rack. Cut into 16 squares. Frost and decorate, if desired.

Makes 16 squares

Festive Franks
[reduced-fat/nut-free]

> 1 can (8 ounces) reduced-fat crescent roll dough
> 5½ teaspoons barbecue sauce
> ⅓ cup finely shredded reduced-fat sharp Cheddar cheese
> 8 fat-free hot dogs
> ¼ teaspoon poppy seeds (optional)
> Additional barbecue sauce (optional)

1. Preheat oven to 350°F. Spray large baking sheet with nonstick cooking spray; set aside.

2. Unroll dough and separate into 8 triangles. Cut each triangle in half lengthwise to make 2 triangles. Lightly spread barbecue sauce over each triangle. Sprinkle with cheese.

3. Cut each hot dog in half; trim off rounded ends. Place one hot dog piece at large end of one dough triangle. Roll up jelly-roll style from wide end. Place point-side down on prepared baking sheet. Sprinkle with poppy seeds, if desired. Repeat with remaining hot dog pieces and dough.

4. Bake 13 minutes or until dough is golden brown. Cool 1 to 2 minutes on baking sheet. Serve with additional barbecue sauce for dipping, if desired. *Makes 16 servings*

Tuna Schooners
[reduced-fat/nut-free]

> 4 (3-ounce) cans water-packed light tuna, drained
> 1 cup finely chopped apple
> ½ cup shredded carrot
> ⅔ cup reduced-fat ranch salad dressing
> 4 English muffins, split and lightly toasted
> 16 triangular-shaped baked whole wheat crackers or triangular-shaped tortilla chips

1. Combine tuna, apple and carrot in medium bowl. Add salad dressing; stir to combine.

2. Spread ¼ of tuna mixture over top of each muffin half. Stand 2 crackers and press firmly into tuna mixture on each muffin half to form 'sails.' *Makes 8 servings*

Crispy Rice Squares [nut-free/reduced-fat]

- **3 tablespoons Dried Plum Purée (recipe follows) or prepared dried plum butter**
- **1 tablespoon butter or margarine**
- **1 package (10 ounces) marshmallows**
- **6 cups crisp rice cereal**
- **Colored nonpareils**

Coat 13×9-inch baking pan with vegetable cooking spray. Heat Dried Plum Purée and butter in Dutch oven or large saucepan over low heat, stirring until butter is melted. Add marshmallows; stir until completely melted. Remove from heat. Stir in cereal until well coated. Spray back of wooden spoon with vegetable cooking spray and pat mixture evenly into prepared pan. Sprinkle with nonpareils. Cool until set. Cut into squares. *Makes 24 squares*

Dried Plum Purée: Combine 1⅓ cups (8 ounces) pitted dried plums and ¼ cup plus 2 tablespoons hot water in container of food processor or blender. Pulse on and off until dried plums are finely chopped and smooth. Store leftovers in a covered container in the refrigerator for up to two months. Makes 1 cup.

Favorite recipe from **California Dried Plum Board**

Make It Special

To make Crispy Rice Squares even more festive, cut out shapes with cookie cutters. Double the recipe to make enough cut out cookies. Use the extra pieces to feed the kids, big and little, at home.

Wacky Cake

[dairy-free/reduced-sugar]

- 1½ **cups all-purpose flour**
- ½ **cup granulated sugar**
- ½ **cup granular sucralose-based sugar substitute**
- 3 **tablespoons cocoa**
- 1 **teaspoon baking soda**
- ½ **teaspoon salt**
- 1 **tablespoon vinegar**
- 3 **tablespoons canola oil**
- 3 **tablespoons unsweetened applesauce**
- 1 **teaspoon vanilla**
- 1 **cup water**

1. Measure flour, sugar, sucralose, cocoa, soda and salt into 8×8-inch baking pan. With finger, poke 4 holes in the dry ingredients.

2. Into the first hole, put the vinegar.

3. Into the second hole, put the oil.

4. Into the third hole, put the applesauce.

5. Into the fourth hole, put the vanilla.

6. Pour the water over all. Mix thoroughly with a fork.

7. Bake at 350°F for 25 minutes or until toothpick inserted in center comes out clean. Serve warm.

Makes 16 servings

Tasty Teaching Time

For an ambitious room mom, this is a fun "counting game" cake. With adult supervision and lots of organization, kids can bake their own cake and practice counting.

Lollipop Sugar Cookies

[nut-free]

1¼ cups granulated sugar
1 Butter Flavor CRISCO® Stick or 1 cup Butter Flavor CRISCO® All-Vegetable Shortening
2 eggs
¼ cup light corn syrup or regular pancake syrup
1 tablespoon vanilla
3 cups all-purpose flour
¾ teaspoon baking powder
½ teaspoon baking soda
½ teaspoon salt
36 flat ice cream sticks
   Any of the following: miniature baking chips, raisins, red hots, nonpareils, colored sugar or nuts

1. Combine sugar and 1 cup shortening in large bowl. Beat at medium speed of electric mixer until well blended. Add eggs, syrup and vanilla; beat until well blended and fluffy.

2. Combine flour, baking powder, baking soda and salt. Add gradually to creamed mixture at low speed until well blended. Wrap dough in plastic wrap. Refrigerate at least 1 hour.

3. Heat oven to 375°F. Place foil on countertop for cooling cookies.

4. Shape dough into 1½-inch balls. Push ice cream stick into center of each ball. Place balls 3 inches apart on ungreased baking sheet. Flatten balls to ½-inch thickness with bottom of greased and floured glass. Decorate as desired; press decorations gently into dough.*

5. Bake at 375°F for 8 to 10 minutes. *Do not overbake.* Cool on baking sheet 2 minutes. Remove cookies to foil to cool completely.

Makes about 36 cookies

Cookies can also be painted before baking. Mix 1 egg yolk and ¼ teaspoon water. Divide into 3 small cups. Add 2 to 3 drops food color to each. Stir. Use clean watercolor brushes to paint designs on cookies.

Cinnamon Apple Chips

[nut-free]

- **2 cups unsweetened apple juice**
- **1 cinnamon stick**
- **2 Washington Red Delicious apples**

1. In large skillet or saucepan, combine apple juice and cinnamon stick; bring to a low boil while preparing apples.

2. With paring knife, slice off ½ inch from tops and bottoms of apples and discard (or eat). Stand apples on either cut end; cut crosswise into ⅛-inch-thick slices, rotating apple as necessary to cut even slices.

3. Drop slices into boiling juice; cook 4 to 5 minutes or until slices appear translucent and lightly golden. Meanwhile, preheat oven to 250°F.

4. With slotted spatula, remove apple slices from juice and pat dry. Arrange slices on wire racks, making sure none overlap. Place racks on middle shelf in oven; bake 30 to 40 minutes until slices are lightly browned and almost dry to touch. Let chips cool on racks completely before storing in airtight container. *Makes about 40 chips*

Tip: There is no need to core apples because boiling in juice for several minutes softens core and removes seeds.

Favorite recipe from **Washington Apple Commission**

Make It Special

Many recipes in this book are also great foods for lunch boxes, after school snacks or at-home parties. Bake some delicious new treats for your family that are sure to command a repeat performance!

Strawberry Oat Mini Muffins

[reduced-sugar]

  1 cup all-purpose flour
  ¾ cup uncooked oat bran cereal
  2½ teaspoons baking powder
  ½ teaspoon baking soda
  ⅛ teaspoon salt
  ¾ cup buttermilk
  ⅓ cup frozen apple juice concentrate, thawed
  ⅓ cup unsweetened applesauce
  ½ teaspoon vanilla
  ¾ cup diced strawberries
  ¼ cup chopped pecans (optional)

1. Preheat oven to 400°F. Spray 24 (1¾-inch) miniature muffin cups with nonstick cooking spray.

2. Combine flour, oat bran, baking powder, baking soda and salt in medium bowl. Whisk together buttermilk, apple juice concentrate, applesauce and vanilla in small bowl.

3. Stir buttermilk mixture into flour mixture until dry ingredients are almost moistened. Fold strawberries and pecans, if desired, into batter just until dry ingredients are moistened. *Do not overmix.*

4. Spoon batter into muffin cups. Bake 17 to 18 minutes or until lightly browned and toothpick inserted into centers comes out clean. Cool in pan on wire rack 5 minutes. Remove muffins to racks. Serve warm or cool completely.

Makes 24 muffins

Snacking Surprise Muffins [nut-free]

1½ cups all-purpose flour
½ cup sugar
1 cup fresh or frozen blueberries
2½ teaspoons baking powder
1 teaspoon ground cinnamon
¼ teaspoon salt
1 egg, beaten
⅔ cup buttermilk
¼ cup margarine or butter, melted
3 tablespoons peach preserves

Topping

1 tablespoon sugar
¼ teaspoon ground cinnamon

1. Preheat oven to 400°F. Line 12 standard (2½-inch) muffin cups with paper liners; set aside.

2. Combine flour, ½ cup sugar, blueberries, baking powder, 1 teaspoon cinnamon and salt in medium bowl. Combine egg, buttermilk and margarine in small bowl. Add to flour mixture; mix just until moistened.

3. Spoon about 1 tablespoon batter into each muffin cup. Drop a scant teaspoonful of preserves into center of batter in each cup; top with remaining batter.

4. Combine 1 tablespoon sugar and ¼ teaspoon cinnamon in small bowl; sprinkle evenly over tops of batter.

5. Bake 18 to 20 minutes or until lightly browned. Remove muffins to wire rack to cool completely.

Makes 12 muffins

Pumpkin Snacker Cakes [nut-free]

¼ cup uncooked old-fashioned or quick oats
¼ cup shredded unsweetened coconut
1 box (18¼ ounces) spice cake mix
1¼ cups water
3 eggs *or* 6 egg whites *or* ¾ cup cholesterol-free egg substitute
1 cup solid-pack pumpkin
½ teaspoon ground nutmeg or apple pie spice
½ teaspoon vanilla, butter and nut flavoring

1. Preheat oven to 325°F. Line 36 (1¾-inch) miniature muffin cups with paper baking cups; set aside.

2. Toast oats and coconut in large nonstick skillet over medium heat 3 to 4 minutes or until coconut starts to brown, stirring constantly. Remove from pan; set aside.

3. Combine cake mix, water and eggs in large mixing bowl. Beat with electric mixer at low speed 30 seconds until moistened. Beat at medium speed 2 minutes, scraping bottom and side of bowl. Add pumpkin, nutmeg and flavoring; beat until well blended.

4. Spoon batter into muffin cups. Sprinkle oat mixture evenly over top of batter. Bake 10 minutes or until toothpick inserted in centers comes out clean. Cool in pans on wire racks 10 minutes.

5. Remove from pans to racks; cool completely. Store in tightly sealed container.   *Makes 36 miniature muffins*

Donut Spice Cakes
[nut-free]

1 package (9 ounces) yellow cake mix
½ cup cold water
2 eggs
½ teaspoon ground cinnamon
¼ teaspoon ground nutmeg
2 teaspoons powdered sugar

1. Preheat oven to 350°F. Lightly grease and flour 10 (½-cup) mini Bundt pan cups.

2. Combine cake mix, water, eggs, cinnamon and nutmeg in medium bowl. Beat with electric mixer at high speed 4 minutes or until well blended.

3. Spoon about ¼ cup batter into each prepared Bundt pan cup. Bake 13 minutes or until toothpicks inserted into centers come out clean and cakes spring back when touched lightly.

4. Cool in pans on wire racks 5 minutes. Remove cakes from pans. Serve warm or at room temperature. Sprinkle with powdered sugar just before serving.

Makes 10 servings

Prep Time: 10 minutes • Bake Time: 13 minutes

Fun Fruit Bites
[nut-free]

16 strawberries
16 banana slices (about 2 bananas)
16 green grapes
64 (2¼-inch) pretzel sticks

Gently push 1 pretzel stick into each piece of fruit. Twist pretzel as you are pushing fruit onto it to keep the pretzel from breaking. Serve as soon as possible to keep pretzels crunchy.

Makes 48 pieces

Peach Gingerbread Muffins

[nut-free/dairy-free]

- 2 cups all-purpose flour
- 2 teaspoons baking powder
- 1 teaspoon ground ginger
- ½ teaspoon salt
- ½ teaspoon ground cinnamon
- ¼ teaspoon ground cloves
- ½ cup sugar
- ½ cup MOTT'S® Chunky Apple Sauce
- ¼ cup MOTT'S® Apple Juice
- ¼ cup GRANDMA'S® Molasses
- 1 egg
- 2 tablespoons vegetable oil
- 1 (16-ounce) can peaches in juice, drained and chopped

1. Preheat oven to 400°F. Line 12 (2½-inch) muffin cups with paper liners or spray with nonstick cooking spray.

2. In large bowl, combine flour, baking powder, ginger, salt and spices.

3. In small bowl, combine sugar, apple sauce, apple juice, molasses, egg and oil.

4. Stir apple sauce mixture into flour mixture just until moistened. Fold in peaches.

5. Spoon batter evenly into prepared muffin cups.

6. Bake 20 minutes or until toothpick inserted in centers comes out clean. Immediately remove from pan; cool on wire rack 10 minutes. Serve warm or cool completely.

Makes 12 muffins

Honey Carrot Snacking Cake

[nut-free]

- ½ cup butter or margarine, softened
- 1 cup honey
- 2 eggs
- 2 cups finely grated carrots
- ½ cup golden raisins
- ⅓ cup chopped nuts (optional)
- ¼ cup orange juice
- 2 teaspoons vanilla
- 1 cup all-purpose flour
- 1 cup whole wheat flour
- 2 teaspoons baking powder
- 1½ teaspoons ground cinnamon
- 1 teaspoon baking soda
- ½ teaspoon salt
- ½ teaspoon ground ginger
- ¼ teaspoon ground nutmeg

Cream butter in large bowl. Gradually beat in honey until light and fluffy. Add eggs, one at a time, beating well after each addition. Combine carrots, raisins, nuts, if desired, orange juice and vanilla in medium bowl. Combine remaining dry ingredients in separate large bowl. Add dry ingredients to creamed mixture alternately with carrot mixture, beginning and ending with dry ingredients. Pour batter into greased 13×9×2-inch pan. Bake at 350°F 35 to 45 minutes or until wooden pick inserted near center comes out clean.

Makes 24 servings

Favorite recipe from **National Honey Board**

Hikers' Bar Cookies

[reduced-fat]

- ¾ **cup all-purpose flour**
- ½ **cup packed brown sugar**
- ½ **cup uncooked quick oats**
- ¼ **cup toasted wheat germ**
- ¼ **cup unsweetened applesauce**
- ¼ **cup margarine or butter, softened**
- ⅛ **teaspoon salt**
- ½ **cup cholesterol-free egg substitute**
- ¼ **cup raisins**
- ¼ **cup dried cranberries**
- ¼ **cup sunflower kernels**
- 1 **tablespoon grated orange peel**
- 1 **teaspoon ground cinnamon**

1. Preheat oven to 350°F. Lightly coat 13×9-inch baking pan with nonstick cooking spray; set aside.

2. Beat flour, sugar, oats, wheat germ, applesauce, margarine and salt in large bowl with electric mixer at medium speed until well blended. Stir in egg substitute, raisins, cranberries, sunflower kernels, orange peel and cinnamon. Spread into pan.

3. Bake 15 minutes or until firm to touch. Cool completely in pan. Cut into 24 squares.

Makes 24 servings

Play It Safe

Plan time for kids to wash their hands before eating. Or, purchase a package of hand wipes for everyone to use before and after the party.

Christmas Mouse Ice Creams

[reduced-sugar]

- 1 quart sugar-free fat-free vanilla ice cream
- 2 packages (4 ounces each) single-serving graham cracker crusts
- 12 sugar-free chocolate sandwich cookies, separated and cream filling removed
- 24 black sugar-free jelly beans
- 12 red sugar-free jelly beans
- 1 to 2 teaspoons chocolate sprinkles

1. Place 1 rounded scoop (about ⅓ cup) ice cream into each crust. Freeze 10 minutes.

2. Press 1 cookie half into each side of ice cream scoops for ears. Decorate with black jelly beans for eyes, red jelly beans for noses and chocolate sprinkles for whiskers. Freeze 10 minutes before serving.

Makes 12 servings

Orange Yogurt Dip for Fresh Fruit

[nut-free/reduced-fat]

- 1 carton (8 ounces) low-fat plain yogurt
- 2 tablespoons honey
  Grated peel of ½ SUNKIST® orange
- 2 SUNKIST® oranges, peeled and segmented
- 1 medium unpeeled apple, sliced*
- 1 medium banana, peeled and cut into chunks*

Sprinkle cut apple and banana with small amount of orange or lemon juice to prevent fruit from darkening.

In small bowl, combine yogurt, honey and orange peel. Serve as dip with oranges, apple and banana.

Makes 4 (2-ounce) servings

Chicken Nuggets with Barbecue Dipping Sauce

[nut-free]

- 1 pound boneless skinless chicken breasts
- ¼ cup all-purpose flour
- ¼ teaspoon salt
- Dash black pepper
- 2 cups crushed reduced-fat baked cheese crackers
- 1 teaspoon dried oregano leaves
- 1 egg white
- 1 tablespoon water
- 3 tablespoons barbecue sauce
- 2 tablespoons all-fruit peach or apricot jam

1. Preheat oven to 400°F. Rinse chicken. Pat dry with paper towels. Cut into 40 (1-inch) pieces.

2. Place flour, salt and pepper in resealable plastic food storage bag. Combine cracker crumbs and oregano in shallow bowl. Whisk together egg white and water in small bowl.

3. Place 6 or 8 chicken pieces in bag with flour mixture; seal bag. Shake until chicken is well coated. Remove chicken from bag; shake off excess flour. Coat all sides of chicken pieces with egg white mixture. Roll in crumb mixture. Place in shallow baking pan. Repeat with remaining chicken pieces. Bake 10 to 13 minutes or until golden brown.

4. Meanwhile, combine barbecue sauce and jam in small saucepan. Cook and stir over low heat until heated through. Serve with chicken nuggets.

5. Place nuggets in disposable aluminum pans. Cover and place in insulated bags to carry to school. Serve immediately or reheat and serve.

Makes 40 pieces

Chicken Nuggets with Barbecue Dipping Sauce ✱ 169

Angelic Cupcakes

[nut-free/reduced-sugar]

   1 **box (16 ounces) angel food cake mix**
1¼ **cups cold water**
   ¼ **teaspoon peppermint extract (optional)**
      Red food coloring
4½ **cups thawed frozen light whipped topping**
      Green food coloring (optional)

1. Preheat oven to 375°F. Line 36 standard (2½-inch) muffin cups with paper liners; set aside.

2. Beat cake mix, water and peppermint extract, if desired, in large bowl with electric mixer at low speed 30 seconds. Increase speed to medium and beat 1 minute.

3. Pour half of batter into medium bowl; carefully stir in 9 drops red food coloring. In each muffin cup, alternate spoonfuls of white and pink batter, filling baking cups ¾ full.

4. Bake 11 minutes or until cupcakes are golden with deep cracks on top. Remove to wire rack. Cool completely.

5. Divide whipped topping between three small bowls. Add 2 drops green food coloring to one bowl of whipped topping; stir gently to combine. Add 2 drops red food coloring to one bowl of whipped topping; stir gently to combine. Frost cupcakes with red, green and white whipped topping as desired. Refrigerate leftovers.

Makes 36 cupcakes

Dainty Digits

[reduced-sugar]

   2 **tablespoons cream cheese**
24 **baby carrots**
24 **almond slices**
      Salsa

Spread small dab of cream cheese on the tip of each baby carrot. Gently press almond slice onto cream cheese to resemble fingernails. Serve on a platter with a bowl of salsa for dipping. *Makes 24 carrots*

Banana Mini Muffins

[nut-free]

2 extra-ripe, medium DOLE® Bananas
⅔ cup brown sugar, packed
1 egg
⅓ cup buttermilk
⅓ cup vegetable oil
1 teaspoon vanilla extract
1¼ cups all-purpose flour
½ cup whole wheat flour
2 teaspoons baking powder
1 teaspoon ground nutmeg
½ teaspoon baking soda
¼ teaspoon salt
¼ cup mini semisweet chocolate pieces, optional

● Purée bananas in blender (1 cup). Beat sugar and egg in large bowl until smooth. Mix in bananas, buttermilk, oil and vanilla.

● Combine flours, baking powder, nutmeg, baking soda and salt in medium bowl; stir into banana mixture with chocolate pieces, if desired, just until moistened.

● Spoon into greased or paper-lined mini muffin pans or regular muffin pans. Bake at 375°F 12 minutes for mini muffins or 17 to 20 minutes for standard muffins. Turn out onto racks to cool.

Makes 48 mini muffins or 12 standard muffins

Blueberry Orange Muffins [nut-free]

1¾ cups all-purpose flour
⅓ cup sugar
2½ teaspoons baking powder
½ teaspoon baking soda
½ teaspoon salt
½ teaspoon ground cinnamon
¾ cup fat-free (skim) milk
1 egg, lightly beaten
¼ cup butter, melted and slightly cooled
3 tablespoons orange juice concentrate, thawed
1 teaspoon vanilla
¾ cup fresh or frozen blueberries, thawed

1. Preheat oven to 400°F. Grease or paper line 12 standard (2½-inch) muffin cups.

2. Combine flour, sugar, baking powder, baking soda, salt and cinnamon in large bowl. Set aside. Beat milk, egg, butter, orange juice concentrate and vanilla in medium bowl on medium speed of electric mixer until well combined. Add milk mixture to dry ingredients. Mix lightly until dry ingredients are barely moistened (mixture will be lumpy). Add blueberries. Stir gently just until berries are evenly distributed.

3. Fill muffin cups ¾ full. Bake 20 to 25 minutes (25 to 30 minutes if using frozen berries) or until toothpick inserted in centers comes out clean. Let cool 5 minutes in pan; remove from pan to wire rack. Serve warm. *Makes 12 muffins*

Confetti Tuna in Celery Sticks

[reduced fat/nut-free]

- 1 (3-ounce) pouch of STARKIST® Premium Albacore or Chunk Light Tuna
- ½ cup shredded red or green cabbage
- ½ cup shredded carrot
- ¼ cup shredded yellow squash or zucchini
- 3 tablespoons reduced-calorie cream cheese, softened
- 1 tablespoon plain low-fat yogurt
- ½ teaspoon dried basil, crushed
  Salt and pepper to taste
- 10 to 12 (4-inch) celery sticks, with leaves if desired

1. In a small bowl toss together tuna, cabbage, carrot and squash. Stir in cream cheese, yogurt and basil. Add salt and pepper to taste. With small spatula spread mixture evenly into celery sticks.

2. Pack in covered plastic containers; refrigerate. Place in insulated bags with frozen ice packs to carry to school.

Makes 10 to 12 servings

Golden Chicken Nuggets

[reduced-fat]

- 1 envelope LIPTON® RECIPE SECRETS® Golden Onion Soup Mix
- ½ cup plain dry bread crumbs
- 1½ pounds boneless, skinless chicken breasts, cut into 2-inch pieces
- 2 tablespoons margarine or butter, melted

1. Preheat oven to 425°F. In small bowl, combine soup mix and bread crumbs. Dip chicken in bread crumb mixture until evenly coated.

2. On lightly greased cookie sheet, arrange chicken; drizzle with margarine.

3. Bake uncovered 15 minutes or until chicken is thoroughly cooked, turning once.

Makes 6 servings

Tip: Also terrific with Lipton® Recipe Secrets® Onion, Onion-Mushroom, or Savory Herb with Garlic Soup Mix.

Rollers & Wraps

For a creative alternative to sweet snacks, fill up the crowd with miniature sandwiches—rolled or wrapped for fun-to-eat, less messy snacks.

Sweet Treat Tortillas

8 (7- to 8-inch) flour tortillas
1 package (8 ounces) Neufchatel cheese, softened
½ cup strawberry or other flavor spreadable fruit or preserves
2 medium bananas, peeled and chopped

1. Spread each tortilla with 1 ounce Neufchatel cheese and 1 tablespoon spreadable fruit; top with ¼ of the banana.

2. Roll up tortillas; wrap individually in plastic wrap or place in covered plastic container. Refrigerate until ready to serve.

3. Place in insulated bags with frozen ice packs to carry to school. To serve, cut each roll crosswise into thirds.   *Makes 24 rolls*

More Sweet Treats: Substitute your favorite chopped fruit for bananas.

Cinnamon-Spice Treats: Omit spreadable fruit and bananas. Mix small amounts of sugar, ground cinnamon and nutmeg to taste into Neufchatel cheese; spread evenly onto tortillas. Top with chopped fruit or raisins, if desired; roll up. Cut crosswise into thirds.

Pizza Snack Cups

 1 can (12 ounces) refrigerated biscuits (10 biscuits)
 ½ pound ground beef
 1 jar (14 ounces) RAGÚ® Pizza Quick® Sauce
 ½ cup shredded mozzarella cheese (about 2 ounces)

1. Preheat oven to 375°F. In muffin pan, evenly press each biscuit in bottom and up side of each cup; chill until ready to fill.

2. In 10-inch skillet, brown ground beef over medium-high heat; drain. Stir in Ragú Pizza Quick Sauce and heat through. Evenly spoon beef mixture into prepared muffin cups. Bake 15 minutes. Sprinkle with cheese and bake an additional 5 minutes or until cheese is melted and biscuits are golden. Let stand 5 minutes. Gently remove pizza cups from muffin pan and serve.   *Makes 10 pizza cups*

Note: Carry pizza cups to school in muffin pans or place cups in covered disposable aluminum pans. Pack in insulated bags to keep warm or reheat in pans at school.

Peanut Butter and Jelly Pizza Sandwiches

 1 English muffin
 2 tablespoons JIF® Creamy Peanut Butter
 2 tablespoons SMUCKER'S® Strawberry Jam
 6 to 8 slices banana
   Chocolate syrup
   Sweetened, flaked coconut (optional)

Split and toast English muffin. Spread JIF® peanut butter on both sides of the English muffin. Spread SMUCKER'S® Strawberry Jam on JIF® peanut butter. Top with banana slices. Drizzle on chocolate syrup to taste. Sprinkle with coconut flakes if desired.   *Makes 2 servings*

Note: Prepare sandwiches with peanut butter and jelly. Place in single layer in covered plastic container. Add bananas and drizzle with chocolate just before serving.

Stuffed Bundles

    1 package (10 ounces) refrigerated pizza dough
    2 ounces lean ham or turkey ham, chopped
    ½ cup (2 ounces) shredded reduced-fat sharp Cheddar cheese

1. Preheat oven to 425°F. Coat nonstick 12-cup muffin pan with nonstick cooking spray.

2. Unroll dough on flat surface; cut into 12 pieces, about 4×3 inch rectangles. Divide ham and cheese between dough rectangles. Bring corners of dough together, pinching to seal. Place, smooth side up, in prepared muffin cups.

3. Bake 10 to 12 minutes or until golden. Cool slightly. Pack in covered disposable aluminum pans. Place in insulated bags to keep warm or reheat and serve.   *Makes 12 bundles*

Kids' Quesadillas

    8 slices American cheese
    8 (10-inch) flour tortillas
    6 tablespoons *French's®* Sweet & Tangy Honey Mustard
    ½ pound thinly sliced deli turkey
    2 tablespoons melted butter
    ¼ teaspoon paprika

1. To prepare 1 quesadilla, arrange 2 slices of cheese on 1 tortilla. Top with one-fourth of the turkey. Spread with *1½ tablespoons* mustard, then top with another tortilla. Prepare 3 more quesadillas with remaining ingredients.

2. Combine butter and paprika. Brush one side of tortilla with butter mixture. Preheat 12-inch nonstick skillet over medium-high heat. Arrange tortilla butter side down and cook 2 minutes. Brush tortilla with butter mixture and turn over. Cook 1½ minutes or until golden brown. Repeat with remaining three quesadillas. Slice into wedges before serving.   *Makes 4 servings*

Note: Carry quesadillas to school in covered disposable aluminum pans. Pack in insulated bags to keep warm.

Rock 'n' Rollers

- 8 (6- to 7-inch) flour tortillas
- 1 package (8 ounces) Neufchâtel cheese, softened
- 2/3 cup peach preserves
- 2 cups (8 ounces) shredded fat-free Cheddar cheese
- 1 cup packed washed fresh spinach leaves
- 6 ounces thinly sliced regular or smoked turkey breast

1. Spread each tortilla evenly with 1 ounce Neufchâtel cheese; cover with thin layer of preserves. Sprinkle with Cheddar cheese.

2. Arrange spinach leaves and turkey over Cheddar cheese. Roll up tortillas; trim ends. Place rollers in covered plastic container. Refrigerate until ready to serve.

3. Pack containers in insulated bags with frozen ice packs. To serve, cut each roller crosswise in half or diagonally into 1-inch pieces.

Makes 16 to 24 roll-up slices

Sassy Salsa Rollers: Substitute salsa for peach preserves and shredded iceberg lettuce for spinach leaves.

Ham 'n' Apple Rollers: Omit peach preserves and spinach leaves. Substitute lean ham slices for turkey. Spread tortillas with Neufchâtel cheese as directed; sprinkle with Cheddar cheese. Top each tortilla with about 2 tablespoons finely chopped apple and 2 ham slices; roll up. Continue as directed.

Play It Safe

Keep hot food hot and cold food cold: 140°F or above for hot food, 40° F or below for cold food. To keep food cool, use an insulated bag with a frozen ice pack. Carry hot food in a thermos or insulated bag.

Pizza Rollers

    2 packages (10 ounces each) refrigerated pizza dough
    1 cup pizza sauce
    36 slices turkey pepperoni
    12 sticks mozzarella cheese

1. Preheat oven to 425°F. Coat baking sheet with nonstick cooking spray.

2. Roll out pizza dough on baking sheet to form 12×9-inch rectangle. Cut pizza dough into 6 (4½×4-inch) rectangles. Repeat with remaining dough. Spread about 1 tablespoon sauce over center third of each rectangle. Top with 3 slices pepperoni and stick of mozzarella cheese. Bring ends of dough together over cheese, pinching to seal. Place seam side down on prepared baking sheet.

3. Bake in center of oven 10 minutes or until golden brown. Cool slightly. Place warm Pizza Rollers in disposable aluminum pans. Pack in insulated bags to carry to school. Either serve immediately or reheat at school.

Makes 12 rollers

Tasty Teaching Time

Sandwiches and snacks are a lot more likely to be eaten if they are served in small sizes. Small portions not only avoid wasting food but encourage students to taste unfamiliar foods that may be less appealing in large servings.

Fantasy Cinnamon Applewiches

8 slices raisin bread
⅔ cup reduced-fat cream cheese
⅓ cup finely chopped unpeeled apple
2 teaspoons sugar
¼ teaspoon ground cinnamon

1. Toast bread. Cut slices into desired shapes using large cookie cutters.

2. Combine cream cheese and apple in small bowl; spread onto toast.

3. Combine sugar and cinnamon in another small bowl; sprinkle evenly over cream cheese mixture. Place sandwiches in covered plastic container; refrigerate. Place containers in insulated bags with frozen ice packs to carry to school.

Makes 8 sandwiches

Corn Dogs

8 hot dogs
8 wooden craft sticks
1 package (about 16 ounces) refrigerated grand-size corn biscuits
⅓ cup French's® Classic Yellow® Mustard
8 slices American cheese, cut in half

1. Preheat oven to 350°F. Insert 1 wooden craft stick halfway into each hot dog; set aside.

2. Separate biscuits. On floured board, press or roll each biscuit into a 7×4-inch oval. Spread *2 teaspoons* mustard lengthwise down center of each biscuit. Top each with 2 pieces of cheese. Place hot dog in center of biscuit. Fold top of dough over end of hot dog. Fold sides towards center enclosing hot dog. Pinch edges to seal.

3. Place corn dogs, seam-side down, on greased baking sheet. Bake 20 to 25 minutes or until golden brown. Cool slightly before serving.

Makes 8 corn dogs

Tip: Corn dogs may be made without wooden craft sticks. Carry to school in disposable aluminum baking pans. Pack in insulated bags. Serve immediately or reheat before serving.

Kids' Wrap

  5 tablespoons Dijon honey mustard
  8 (8-inch) fat-free flour tortillas
  8 slices reduced-fat American cheese, cut in half
  1 pound thinly sliced fat-free oven-roasted turkey breast
  1 cup shredded carrot (about 1 medium)
 12 romaine or leafy green lettuce leaves, washed and torn
      into bite-size pieces

1. Spread about 2 teaspoons mustard evenly over one tortilla.

2. Top with 2 cheese halves, half of turkey, half of shredded carrots and half of torn lettuce.

3. Roll up tortilla and cut in half. Repeat with remaining ingredients. Wrap tortillas individually in plastic wrap or place in covered plastic container. Refrigerate. Carry to school in insulated bags with frozen ice packs.

Makes 16 pieces

Tasty Teaching Time

Food wrapped in edible bundles always tastes twice as delightful. Flour tortilla wraps like Kids' Wrap are a child-friendly way to contribute toward the recommended servings of fruits and vegetables for a day.

Dizzy Dogs

- 2 packages (8 breadsticks or 11 ounces each) refrigerated breadsticks
- 2 packages (16 ounces each) hot dogs (16 hot dogs)
- 2 egg whites
  Sesame and/or poppy seeds
  Mustard, ketchup and barbecue sauce (optional)

1. Preheat oven to 375°F.

2. Using 1 breadstick for each, wrap hot dogs with dough in spiral pattern. Brush breadstick dough with egg white and sprinkle with sesame and/or poppy seeds. Place on ungreased baking sheet.

3. Bake 12 to 15 minutes or until light golden brown. Cool slightly. Place in covered disposable aluminum pans. Carry to school in insulated bags. Serve immediately or reheat and serve with condiments for dipping, if desired. *Makes 16 hot dogs*

Taco Cups

- 1 pound lean ground beef, turkey or pork
- 1 package (1 ounce) LAWRY'S® Taco Spices & Seasonings
- 1¼ cups water
- ¼ cup salsa
- 2 packages (8 ounces each) refrigerator biscuits
- ½ cup (2 ounces) shredded cheddar cheese

In medium skillet, brown ground beef until crumbly; drain fat. Stir in Taco Spices & Seasonings and water. Bring to a boil; reduce heat to low and cook, uncovered, 10 minutes. Stir in salsa. Separate biscuits and press each biscuit into an ungreased muffin cup. Spoon equal amounts of meat mixture into each muffin cup; sprinkle each with cheese. Bake, uncovered, in 350°F oven for 12 minutes.

Makes about 16 taco cups

Note: Cool cups slightly in pans. Cover and pack muffin pans in insulated bags to carry to school. Serve immediately or reheat in pans.

Dem Bones

2 packages (6 ounces) sliced ham
1½ cups (6 ounces) shredded Swiss cheese
½ cup mayonnaise
2 tablespoons sweet pickle relish
1 teaspoon mustard
½ teaspoon black pepper
12 slices white bread

1. Place ham in bowl of food processor or blender; process until ground. Combine ham, cheese, mayonnaise, relish, mustard and pepper in small bowl until well blended.

2. Cut out 12 bone shapes from bread using 3½-inch bone-shaped cookie cutter or sharp knife. Spread half of "bones" with 2 tablespoons ham mixture; top with remaining "bones." Either place sandwiches in covered plastic container or wrap individually. Refrigerate until ready to serve. Carry to school in insulated bags with frozen ice packs.

Makes 12 miniature sandwiches

Make It Special

Fun-shaped foods makes eating more appetizing. Make miniature sandwiches using other shaped cookie cutters like stars or apples.

Rainbow Spirals

- 4 (10-inch) flour tortillas (assorted flavors and colors)
- 4 tablespoons *French's*® Mustard (any flavor)
- ½ pound (about 8 slices) thinly sliced deli roast beef, bologna or turkey
- 8 slices American, provolone or Muenster cheese
  Fancy Party Toothpicks

1. Spread each tortilla with *1 tablespoon* mustard. Layer with meat and cheeses, dividing evenly.

2. Roll up jelly-roll style; secure with toothpicks and cut into thirds. Arrange on platter. *Makes 12 roll-up slices*

Prep Time: 10 minutes

Note: For classroom treats, eliminate the toothpicks. Wrap each roll securely in plastic wrap. Refrigerate before cutting to serve.

Monster Finger Sandwiches

- 2 cans (11 ounces) refrigerated breadstick dough (12 breadsticks)
  Mustard
- 24 slices deli ham, cut into ½-inch strips
- 8 slices Monterey Jack cheese, cut into ½-inch strips
- 2 egg yolks, lightly beaten
  Assorted food colorings

1. Preheat oven to 350°F. Place 6 breadsticks on ungreased baking sheets. Spread with mustard as desired. Divide ham strips evenly among breadsticks, placing over mustard. Repeat with cheese. Top with remaining 6 breadsticks. Gently stretch top dough over filling; press dough together to seal.

2. Score knuckle and nail lines into each sandwich using sharp knife. Do not cut completely through dough. Tint egg yolk with food coloring as desired. Paint nail with egg yolk mixture.

3. Bake on lower oven rack 12 to 13 minutes or just until golden. Let cool slightly. Serve warm or cool completely. *Makes 12 servings*

Rainbow Spirals ✿ 195

Cinnamon-Raisin Roll-Ups

1 package (8 ounces) reduced-fat cream cheese, softened
1 cup shredded carrots
½ cup golden or regular raisins
2 tablespoons honey
½ teaspoon ground cinnamon
8 (7- to 8-inch) whole wheat or regular flour tortillas
16 thin apple wedges (optional)

1. Combine cream cheese, carrot, raisins, honey and cinnamon in small bowl; mix well.

2. Spread tortillas evenly with cream cheese mixture, leaving ½-inch border around edge of each tortilla. Place 2 apple wedges down center of each tortilla, if desired; roll up. Wrap in plastic wrap. Refrigerate until ready to serve.   *Makes 8 roll-ups*

Save Time

For extra convenience, prepare roll-ups the night before. Pack in covered plastic containers and refrigerate. At the same time put small juice boxes in the freezer. In the morning, pack roll-ups along with frozen juice boxes in coolers. The juice boxes will thaw by serving time and will keep the snacks cold in the meantime.

Chicken Tortilla Roll-Ups

    1 package (8 ounces) light cream cheese, softened
    ¼ cup mayonnaise
    2 tablespoons Dijon mustard (optional)
    ½ teaspoon black pepper
    6 (10- to 12-inch) flour tortillas
    2 cups finely chopped cooked chicken (optional)
 1½ cups shredded or finely chopped carrot
 1½ cups finely chopped green bell pepper

1. Combine cream cheese, mayonnaise, mustard and black pepper in small bowl; stir until well blended.

2. Spread cream cheese mixture evenly onto each tortilla leaving ½-inch border. Divide chicken, if desired, carrot and bell pepper evenly over cream cheese leaving 1½-inch border on cream cheese mixture at one end of each tortilla.

3. Roll up each tortilla jelly-roll fashion. Refrigerate until ready to serve. Cut each roll into 1½-inch-thick slices.   *Makes 24 to 30 roll-up slices*

Make It Special

Wrap rolls in plastic wrap and refrigerate for several hours for easier slicing and to allow flavors to blend. For other flavor variations, leave out the chicken for veggie roll-ups or substitute other meats for chicken like chopped turkey or ham.

Last Minute Treats

Oh my! You promised to bring classroom treats and just ran out of time. This chapter saves the day with tasty, easy-to-prepare treats.

Chocolate Cherry Cupcakes

    1 package (about 18 ounces) devil's food cake mix
 1⅓ cups water
    3 eggs
  ½ cup sour cream
  ⅓ cup oil
    1 cup dried cherries
    1 container (16 ounces) buttercream frosting, divided
  25 drops green food coloring
  11 maraschino cherries, stems removed and cherries cut in half

1. Preheat oven to 350°F. Line 22 standard (2½-inch) muffin cups with paper baking cups.

2. Beat cake mix, water, eggs, sour cream and oil in large bowl 30 seconds at low speed of electric mixer until just blended. Beat on medium speed 2 minutes or until smooth. Fold in dried cherries.

3. Fill muffin cups ¾ full with batter. Bake 20 to 24 minutes or until wooden pick inserted into centers comes out clean. Cool in pan on wire rack 10 minutes. Remove from pan to wire rack; cool completely.

4. Place ¼ cup frosting in small bowl with food coloring. Stir to combine; set aside.

5. Frost cupcakes with remaining white frosting. Place 1 cherry half, cut-side down, onto each cupcake. Place green frosting in piping bag fitted with writing tip. Pipe a stem and leaf onto each cupcake.

Makes 22 cupcakes

Angel Almond Cupcakes

   1 **package DUNCAN HINES® Angel Food Cake Mix**
1¼ **cups water**
   2 **teaspoons almond extract**
   1 **container DUNCAN HINES® Wild Cherry Vanilla Frosting**

1. Preheat oven to 350°F.

2. Combine cake mix, water and almond extract in large mixing bowl. Beat at low speed with electric mixer until moistened. Beat at medium speed for 1 minute. Line medium muffin pans with paper baking cups. Fill muffin cups two-thirds full. Bake at 350°F for 20 to 25 minutes or until golden brown, cracked and dry on top. Remove from muffin pans. Cool completely. Frost with frosting.

Makes 30 to 32 cupcakes

Candy Corn Crispie Treats

  ½ **cup (1 stick) butter or margarine**
  9 **cups miniature marshmallows**
10 **cups chocolate crispy rice cereal**
  2 **cups candy corn**
  ¾ **cup miniature chocolate chips**
    Assorted candy pumpkins

1. Melt butter in large saucepan over medium heat. Add marshmallows and stir until smooth.

2. Pour cereal, candy corn and chocolate chips into large bowl. Pour butter and marshmallows over cereal mixture, stirring quickly to coat. For best results, use a wooden spoon sprayed with nonstick cooking spray.

3. Spread mixture on large buttered jelly-roll pan, pressing out evenly with buttered hands. While still warm, press on candy pumpkins spaced about 1½ inches apart.

4. Cool, then cut into squares.

Makes about 48 squares

Double Chocolate Snack Cake

1 package DUNCAN HINES® Moist Deluxe® Devil's Food Cake Mix
1 cup white chocolate chips, divided
½ cup semisweet chocolate chips

1. Preheat oven to 350°F. Grease and flour 13×9-inch pan.

2. Prepare cake mix as directed on package. Stir in ½ cup white chocolate chips and semisweet chocolate chips. Pour into prepared pan. Bake at 350°F for 35 to 40 minutes or until toothpick inserted in center comes out clean. Remove from oven; sprinkle top with remaining ½ cup white chocolate chips. Serve warm or cool completely in pan.

Makes 12 to 16 servings

Tip: For a special treat, serve cake with a scoop of vanilla ice cream or whipped cream garnished with chocolate chips.

Crispy Cocoa Bars

¼ cup (½ stick) margarine
¼ cup HERSHEY¡S Cocoa
5 cups miniature marshmallows
5 cups crisp rice cereal

1. Spray 13×9×2-inch pan with vegetable cooking spray.

2. Melt margarine in large saucepan over low heat; stir in cocoa and marshmallows. Cook over low heat, stirring constantly, until marshmallows are melted and mixture is smooth and well blended. Continue cooking 1 minute, stirring constantly. Remove from heat.

3. Add cereal; stir until coated. Lightly spray spatula with vegetable cooking spray; press mixture into prepared pan. Cool completely. Cut into bars.

Makes 24 bars

Conversation Heart Cereal Treats

20 large marshmallows
2 tablespoons margarine or butter
3 cups frosted oat cereal with marshmallow bits
16 large conversation hearts

1. Line 8- or 9-inch square pan with aluminum foil, leaving 2-inch overhangs on 2 sides. Generously grease or spray with nonstick cooking spray.

2. Melt marshmallows and margarine in medium saucepan over medium heat 3 minutes or until melted and smooth, stirring constantly. Remove from heat.

3. Add cereal; stir until completely coated. Spread in prepared pan; press evenly onto bottom using greased rubber spatula. Press heart candies into top of treats while still warm, evenly spacing to allow 1 heart per bar. Let cool 10 minutes. Using foil overhangs as handles, remove treats from pan. Cut into 16 bars. *Makes 16 bars*

Prep and Cook Time: 18 minutes

Make It Special

Select novelty candles in shapes of numerals, cartoon figures, and also novelty candle holders to quickly decorate a cakes and cupcakes.

Berry Surprise Cupcakes

1 package DUNCAN HINES® Moist Deluxe® White Cake Mix
3 egg whites
1⅓ cups water
2 tablespoons vegetable oil
3 sheets (0.5 ounce each) strawberry chewy fruit snacks
1 container DUNCAN HINES® Vanilla Frosting
2 pouches (0.9 ounce each) chewy fruit snack shapes,
   for garnish (optional)

1. Preheat oven to 350°F. Place 24 (2½-inch) paper liners in muffin cups.

2. Combine cake mix, egg whites, water and oil in large bowl. Beat at low speed with electric mixer until moistened. Beat at medium speed 2 minutes. Fill each liner half full with batter.

3. Cut 3 fruit snack sheets into 9 equal pieces. (You will have 3 extra squares.) Place each fruit snack piece on top of batter in each cup. Pour remaining batter equally over each. Bake at 350°F for 18 to 23 minutes or until toothpick inserted in center comes out clean. Cool in pans 5 minutes. Remove to cooling racks. Cool completely. Frost cupcakes with Vanilla frosting. Decorate with fruit snack shapes, if desired.   *Makes 24 cupcakes*

Make It Special

If you are in a rush, make a Berry Surprise Cake. Prepare the cake following the package directions. Pour half the batter into a prepared 13×9×2-inch pan. Place 4 fruit snack sheets evenly on top. Pour the remaining batter over all. Bake and cool as directed on the package. Frost and decorate as described above.

Hershey's Easy Chocolate Cracker Snacks

- 1⅔ cups (10-ounce package) HERSHEY'S Mint Chocolate Chips*
- 2 cups (12-ounce package) HERSHEY'S Semi-Sweet Chocolate Chips
- 2 tablespoons shortening (do not use butter, margarine, spread or oil)
- 60 to 70 round buttery crackers (about one-half 1-pound box)

2 cups (11.5-ounce package) HERSHEY'S Milk Chocolate Chips and ¼ teaspoon pure peppermint extract can be substituted for mint chocolate chips.

1. Line several trays or cookie sheets with waxed paper.

2. Place mint chocolate chips, chocolate chips and shortening in large microwave-safe bowl. Microwave at HIGH (100%) 1 minute; stir. Continue heating 30 seconds at a time, stirring after each heating, until chips are melted and mixture is smooth when stirred.

3. Drop crackers into chocolate mixture one at a time. Using tongs, push cracker into chocolate so that it is covered completely. (If chocolate begins to thicken, reheat 10 to 20 seconds in microwave.) Remove from chocolate, tapping lightly on edge of bowl to remove excess chocolate. Place on prepared tray. Refrigerate until chocolate hardens, about 20 minutes. For best results, store tightly covered in refrigerator. *Makes about 66 snacks*

Peanut Butter and Milk Chocolate: Use 1⅔ cups (10-ounce package) REESE'S® Peanut Butter Chips, 2 cups (11.5-ounce package) HERSHEY'S Milk Chocolate Chips and 2 tablespoons shortening. Proceed as above.

Chocolate Raspberry: Use 1⅔ cups (10-ounce package) HERSHEY'S Raspberry Chips, 2 cups (11.5-ounce package) HERSHEY'S Milk Chocolate Chips and 2 tablespoons shortening. Proceed as above.

White Chip and Toffee: Melt 1⅔ cups (10-ounce package) HERSHEY'S Premier White Chips and 1 tablespoon shortening. Dip Crackers; before coating hardens sprinkle with SKOR® English Toffee Bits or HEATH® BITS 'O BRICKLE® Almond Toffee Bits.

Ice Cream Cone Cupcakes

  1 **package (18¼ ounces) white cake mix**
        plus ingredients to prepare mix
  2 **tablespoons nonpareils***
24 **flat-bottomed ice cream cones**
      Vanilla and chocolate frosting
      Candies and other decorations

Nonpareils are tiny, round, brightly colored sprinkles used for cake and cookie decorating.

Preheat oven to 350°F. Prepare cake mix according to package directions. Stir in nonpareils. Spoon ¼ cup batter into each ice cream cone. Stand cones in 13×9-inch baking pan or muffin tins. Bake cones until toothpick inserted into centers of cakes comes out clean, about 20 minutes. Cool on wire racks. Frost each filled cone. Decorate as desired. *Makes 24 cupcakes*

Note: Cupcakes are best served the day they are prepared. Store loosely covered.

Glazed Donut Cookies

  2 **packages (18 ounces each) refrigerated oatmeal raisin**
        cookie dough in squares or rounds (12 count)
      Prepared white or chocolate frosting
      Assorted white or chocolate frosting

Preheat oven to 350°F. Grease 24 standard (2½-inch) muffin pan cups. Remove dough from wrapper. Separate dough into 12 pieces; let stand at room temperature about 15 minutes. Shape each dough piece into 12-inch-long rope on lightly floured surface. Coil ropes into muffin cups, leaving centers open. Bake 12 minutes; remove from oven and re-shape center hole with round handle of wooden spoon. Return to oven; bake 3 to 4 minutes or until set. Remove from oven; reshape holes, if necessary. Cool in pan 4 minutes; transfer cookies to wire racks to cool completely. Spread frosting over cookies; decorate with sprinkles. *Makes 24 cookies*

Brownie Gems

  1 package DUNCAN HINES® Chocolate Lover's® Double
    Fudge Brownie Mix
  2 eggs
  2 tablespoons water
  ⅓ cup vegetable oil
  28 miniature peanut butter cup or chocolate kiss candies
  1 container of your favorite Duncan Hines frosting

1. Preheat oven to 350°F. Spray (1¾-inch) mini-muffin pans with vegetable cooking spray or line with foil baking cups.

2. Combine brownie mix, fudge packet from mix, eggs, water and oil in large bowl. Stir with spoon until well blended, about 50 strokes. Drop 1 heaping teaspoonful of batter into each muffin cup; top with candy. Cover candy with more batter. Bake at 350°F for 15 to 17 minutes.

3. Cool 5 minutes. Carefully loosen brownies from pan. Remove to wire racks to cool completely. Frost and decorate as desired.

Makes 28 brownie gems

Number One Cake

  1 (13×9-inch) cake
  1 (19×13-inch) cake board, cut in half crosswise and covered
  1½ cups prepared white frosting
    Yellow food coloring
    Assorted colored candies

1. Trim top and sides of cake. Draw a number 1 pattern on 13×9-inch piece of waxed paper. Cut pattern out and place on cake. Cut out cake around the pattern; place on prepared cake board. Reserve extra cake for another use.

2. Tint frosting yellow; frost cake. Decorate with assorted candies as desired.

Makes 16 servings

Sugar-and-Spice Twists

1 tablespoon sugar
¼ teaspoon ground cinnamon
1 package (6-count) refrigerated breadsticks

1. Preheat oven to 350°F. Spray baking sheet with nonstick cooking spray; set aside.

2. Combine sugar and cinnamon in shallow dish or plate; set aside.

3. Divide breadstick dough into 6 pieces. Roll each piece into 12-inch rope. Roll in sugar-cinnamon mixture. Twist into pretzel shape. Place on prepared baking sheet. Bake 15 to 18 minutes or until lightly browned. Remove from baking sheet. Cool 5 minutes. Serve warm.

Makes 6 servings

Hint: Use colored sugar sprinkles in place of the sugar in this recipe for a fun 'twist' of color that's perfect for holidays, birthdays or simple everyday celebrations.

Quick & Easy Pumpkin Cupcakes

1 package (18.25 ounces) spice cake mix
1 can (15 ounces) LIBBY'S® 100% Pure Pumpkin
3 large eggs
⅓ cup vegetable oil
⅓ cup water
1 container (16 ounces) prepared cream cheese or vanilla frosting
Assorted sprinkles

PREHEAT oven to 350°F. Paper-line or grease 24 muffin cups.

BLEND cake mix, pumpkin, eggs, vegetable oil and water in large mixer bowl until moistened. Beat on medium speed for 2 minutes. Pour batter into prepared muffin cups, filling ¾ full.

BAKE for 18 to 23 minutes or until wooden pick inserted in centers comes out clean. Cool in pan on wire rack for 10 minutes; remove to wire racks to cool completely. Spread cupcakes with frosting. Decorate as desired.

Makes 24 cupcakes

The publisher would like to thank the companies and organizations listed below for the use of their recipes and photographs in this publication.

California Dried Plum Board

Cherry Marketing Institute

Dole Food Company, Inc.

Duncan Hines® and Moist Deluxe® are registered trademarks of Aurora Foods Inc.

Hawaiian Punch® is a registered trademark of Mott's, LLP

Hershey Foods Corporation

The Hidden Valley® Food Products Company

JOLLY TIME® Pop Corn

Keebler® Company

Lawry's® Foods

© Mars, Incorporated 2004

Mauna La'i® is a registered trademark of Mott's, LLP

Mott's® is a registered trademark of Mott's, LLP

National Honey Board

Nestlé USA

Reckitt Benckiser Inc.

Reddi-wip® is a registered trademark of ConAgra Brands, Inc.

The J.M. Smucker Company

SPLENDA® is a trademark of McNeil PPC, Inc.

StarKist Seafood Company

The Sugar Association, Inc.

Reprinted with permission of Sunkist Growers, Inc.

Unilever Bestfoods North America

Washington Apple Commission

METRIC CONVERSION CHART

VOLUME MEASUREMENTS (dry)

$^1/_8$ teaspoon = 0.5 mL
$^1/_4$ teaspoon = 1 mL
$^1/_2$ teaspoon = 2 mL
$^3/_4$ teaspoon = 4 mL
1 teaspoon = 5 mL
1 tablespoon = 15 mL
2 tablespoons = 30 mL
$^1/_4$ cup = 60 mL
$^1/_3$ cup = 75 mL
$^1/_2$ cup = 125 mL
$^2/_3$ cup = 150 mL
$^3/_4$ cup = 175 mL
1 cup = 250 mL
2 cups = 1 pint = 500 mL
3 cups = 750 mL
4 cups = 1 quart = 1 L

VOLUME MEASUREMENTS (fluid)

1 fluid ounce (2 tablespoons) = 30 mL
4 fluid ounces ($^1/_2$ cup) = 125 mL
8 fluid ounces (1 cup) = 250 mL
12 fluid ounces (1$^1/_2$ cups) = 375 mL
16 fluid ounces (2 cups) = 500 mL

WEIGHTS (mass)

$^1/_2$ ounce = 15 g
1 ounce = 30 g
3 ounces = 90 g
4 ounces = 120 g
8 ounces = 225 g
10 ounces = 285 g
12 ounces = 360 g
16 ounces = 1 pound = 450 g

DIMENSIONS

$^1/_{16}$ inch = 2 mm
$^1/_8$ inch = 3 mm
$^1/_4$ inch = 6 mm
$^1/_2$ inch = 1.5 cm
$^3/_4$ inch = 2 cm
1 inch = 2.5 cm

OVEN TEMPERATURES

250°F = 120°C
275°F = 140°C
300°F = 150°C
325°F = 160°C
350°F = 180°C
375°F = 190°C
400°F = 200°C
425°F = 220°C
450°F = 230°C

BAKING PAN SIZES

Utensil	Size in Inches/Quarts	Metric Volume	Size in Centimeters
Baking or Cake Pan (square or rectangular)	$8 \times 8 \times 2$	2 L	$20 \times 20 \times 5$
	$9 \times 9 \times 2$	2.5 L	$23 \times 23 \times 5$
	$12 \times 8 \times 2$	3 L	$30 \times 20 \times 5$
	$13 \times 9 \times 2$	3.5 L	$33 \times 23 \times 5$
Loaf Pan	$8 \times 4 \times 3$	1.5 L	$20 \times 10 \times 7$
	$9 \times 5 \times 3$	2 L	$23 \times 13 \times 7$
Round Layer Cake Pan	$8 \times 1^1/_2$	1.2 L	20×4
	$9 \times 1^1/_2$	1.5 L	23×4
Pie Plate	$8 \times 1^1/_4$	750 mL	20×3
	$9 \times 1^1/_4$	1 L	23×3
Baking Dish or Casserole	1 quart	1 L	—
	1$^1/_2$ quart	1.5 L	—
	2 quart	2 L	—